Before dawn
we hear the white birds
departing

All day
their shadows
glide
across the grass

You touch my hair
beneath the trees

and talk of steeple bells
and journeys

—Judith Anne Greenberg
    Flock

floating island

Special thanks to the
California Arts Council
for their support and encouragement
and to the
Ariete Foundation of San Francisco

"Touching" by Gino Clays Sky is from *Jonquil Rose,* published by Five Trees Press;
"Potatoes and Rosehips" was first published as a broadside, also from Five Tress
Press.

The four Kabir poems on pp. 42–45 are from *The Fish in the Sea Is Not Thirsty,*
published by Lillabulero Press and subsequently reprinted by Rainbow Bridge.
They are used here with Robert Bly's permission.

"Just Sitting" by John Read was first published in *Beatitude 24.*

The two poems by Lawrence Ferlinghetti are included in his most recent work,
Who Are We Now? published by New Directions. They are used here with the
author's permission.

Many of the poems by Aram Saroyan are from *O My Generation and Other Poems,*
published by Blackberry Books, Bolinas.

Printed at the West Coast Print Center, Berkeley, California
Typeset by Michael Sykes

⊕ FLOATING ISLAND PUBLICATIONS

Floating Island II: Library of Congress No. 76-6871; published by Floating Island
Publications, P.O. Box 516, Point Reyes Station, California 94956. Subscription
rate is $10/two issues, $16/four issues. Unless otherwise noted, all rights revert to
authors upon request. Please address all inquiries and correspondence to
Michael Sykes, Editor, Floating Island Publications. All material submitted for
consideration should be accompanied by a stamped, self-addressed envelope.
Floating Island Publications is a member of COSMEP and COSMEP-WEST,
orginizations with support and encourage the development of small presses.

floating island II

Michael Sykes
EDITOR

Howard Jacobsen
GRAPHIC DESIGN

FRONT AND BACK COVERS:
Photographs by Thomas Weir

ADDITIONAL ILLUSTRATIONS:
Colleen Kelley, pp. 2, 3, 182, 183
Elia, pp. 18, 24, 25, 134
Inez Storer, pp. 34, 35, 36, 37, 39
Dhyana Greenberger, pp. 41, 42, 43, 78, 169
Carol Snow, pp. 44, 45, 73
Art Rogers, p. 67
Michael Sykes, p. 71
David Bunnett, pp. 107, 108, 109, 111, 112, 113
Cliff Pollock, p. 133
David Lubin, p. 137
Strawberry Saroyan, pp. 140, 141
Gailyn Saroyan, p. 142
Brenda Rose, pp, 28, 30, 31, 165, 166, 167

Morgan Alexander

FORMING CIRCLES
for Stella

We miss each other when we are too near.
When we are far, we see each other clear.
  Dilys Laing, *Let Me Hold You Far*

And for the first time I've been seeing
the things I'd never noticed about you
and for the first time I'm discovering
the things I used to treasure about you.
  Don McLean, *Winterwood*

Compassion is environmental generosity.
  Chogyam Trungpa, Rinpoche

· 1 ·
Coming to Meet

milk runs from my breasts

we have lived here before

knowing darkness
a green balloon this planet

your mouth is still in sleep

surfaces join to separate

the nipples warming brown

hair stringing up your belly

that distance from your neck

winter violets, lavender

across my eyes

i am mother and child

spirits born age after age

the sun goes south in winter

fascination kills reality

hilly breasts softening

hard in the water

forming circles to meet

to your genitals

scent the air, alchemical

at the place of arrival.

· 2 ·

The Arousing (Shock, Thunder)

o mother, if you had once touched me.
o mother, if I had once touched you.
  Charles Olson, *As the Dead Prey Upon Us*

it's hard to get rid of someone
who
doesn't want
to go away.

you tried.
seven times.
seven is the number of the young light.

i think i don't know
what love is.

i came alone into this world
and
experience my aloneness.

i was a commodity
bought by my parents.
sometimes i felt like
ten shares of Anaconda Copper.

i am still afraid
of the dark.

i keep myself
my own child.

sitting in the second to the last row
at the saturday matinee
stuffing popcorn and good 'n plenties
down my gullet
i wondered when someone
would touch me
touch me
someone touch me
love me
love me someone please someone
anyone is there anyone

i hear myself screaming

and no one heard.

· 3 ·

Gathering Together

the sun was only a thought.

grey morning light
kept February distances
blanketing
the diamond starry
and falling snow
in time

in time
refining the alchemy of blood
a tarnished rider
among bending stars
i cry alone, horseless
on the chill mountain.

my shadow falls.

and the child in me is dying
abandoning through light
the little words in little books
the need for despair

i have hidden my fears
from myself
like matches, knives
pieces of string
i carried in my childhood pockets

we come and go
passing in the dark
touching each other
as if for the first time
always
a momentary throttle in the blood.

where do you travel
my child my woman
to that vision
as old and smooth
as the hills.

the spirit returns home
no matter the journey
home to the clan
gathering together
in the slow and only silence.

· 4 ·
Vision

the applauding rain
invades the grotto
somewhere beyond the darkness.
even now it dampens
unashamed and thinning.

that smell of lavender
leavens the pebbles
filmy, scalloped.

breathing into candled sleep
your hair
wheat-fallen and luminous
shoulders my arm.
there is comfort in dreaming.

the clues arch to the stars
in secret.

· 5 ·

in the second grade
i played the witch in hansel and gretel.
i wanted to play gretel
because she was beautiful.
susie robinson played gretel.

and mrs. olsen pointed
her red finger at me
and said
"judy you're playing the witch."

and i got stuck in the cardboard oven
during the show
my eight-year-old ass
in the audience's face.
all my friends laughed.

it was then i knew
that being a witch
made you an outcast.
a position of power.

but it was painful, lonely
to be cast out,
left, stranded.

i was born with a silver spoon
and
no nourishment.

i am hansel and gretel
the good witch
the Fairy Princess
Prince Charming
the frog
Cinderella
Amelia Earhardt
Electra
Horatio Kent the Fool
Jeanne d'Arc
Bridget Bishop
Pocohontas
Emily Dickinson
Florence Chadwick
Dale Arden
Rita Hayworth
and
Cornel Wilde.

· 6 ·

who among us
has not heard
the sound of death
running

dared turn to look
over the left shoulder
feeling warm air behind the ear
a slight breath on the spine.

the crows blacken
winter's calligraphy.

· 7 ·

i cannot
tell you
how i feel
sometimes
i do not
know
my
self

its dark
in here
i get lost
running
down my own
rabbit holes.

i love you
more than

there are
no words
to tell

you have beautiful eyes
i see myself in you

you are a still pool.

· 8 ·

last summer
i bought a silver necklace in Berkeley
a denim coat on Haight Street
and i wore my California dream
to Woodstock
and it choked me

that vision of the homeland
eucalyptus fog thickening
into the Pacific
the sun embracing
healing springs at Big Sur
won't keep me warm enough in Woodstock.

nothing ever looks
like
what it is.

deep into february
no turning back now
the cold in my bones
reliable
i surrender to winter's apparency.

disguise as certain
and deceptive
as the snow

i come to reveal myself
against the circus of winter
the cold impassable roads
flooded basement frozen water pipes
creosote in the woodstove
and my car engine freezes
when it goes to twenty below.

i come to winter
which gives me license
only to
grow.

· 9 ·

as a writer i write entirely with my eyes.
    Gertrude Stein

nobody makes a living as a poet
nobody
few
want to know
the truth

writing is about
telling the truth

putting on paper
exactly what you see
what you notice

i talk too much

i have confused talking with writing
the more i write
the less i talk

poetry is about
honesty love beauty

keats was right

· 10 ·

this time
electra
the real catharsis

no more masquerades
underneath the house floor
waiting to go on stage
at lincoln center
in the dying city
thinking i was somewhere.

looking out into red and black
at all those dead faces
so dead
i could not stand to look anymore.

it was like looking at myself
all the time.

you have beautiful eyes
i see myself in you.

you are a still pool.

· 11 ·

Contemplation

i am the gentle wind
sleeping chill
in the pale web of sunset
a wildness in the veins
as if i dreamed too long.

embracing the earth
between ablution and sacrifice
painting my breasts
tips of yellow dust
tap from my crown's fingers
connecting the auras

i know i am home.

frozen in the deep hills
the world stops.

we quiet the night
clearing the space
behind the eyes.

how still you are
as i am still
at the foot of the mountain.

· 12 ·

to separate distances
of winter
clarifies focus.

how do i see myself
if i'm always
looking at you.
love is no excuse.

a flash of light
across the retina
blinks at arrival
the point
where time and i
converge
splitting the barrier
of absence.

the corners of the mouth
provide nourishment.

· 13 ·
Return (The Turning Point)

the seasons are healing.
solitude sickness pleasure
brown mountains are healing
sun in the sky
summer's heat
touch
these have healed me.

fire air earth water
the elements are healing.

ordinary love.

> *the winter solstice brings*
> *victory of light.*

i am becoming my art.

> *the time of darkness is gone.*
> *on the seventh day*
> *comes return.*

the receptive earth
the arousing thunder.
shock.

to approach is to move away.
i come to myself
to come to you.
that's ordinary love.

return to health after sickness
pleasure after pain
work after confusion
companions after solitude
compassion after greed
love after fear.

return with care
at the beginning.

return leads to flowering.

i am the seasons
forming circles
i am the elements.

and the child in me is dying.

you have beautiful eyes.

Entering Pisces, 1976
Woodstock, New York

Gino Clays Sky

RIDE OUT THE MOON MY BROTHER

The Wolf is the brother to the rabbit,
The Bow is the mother to the arrow.
The Rain and the Sun are fathers to the dream,
The Wind is the sister to the tongue.

My vision is the brother to my dreams.

I choose the path through the forests,
turning away from the freeways, and the voices of warriors.

You are my brother as the mountain is my brother
reaching for the sun
covered with crevasses and vertical walls
calling me to share your joy
with ecstasy and death hidden within your mystery.

Please don't call me brother
without our dream being the same dream
as the spiritual song of our journey.

Please don't call me brother
unless the lightning has joined our hearts together
and we have danced with joy in the beginning
of our first creation.

Please don't call me brother
unless the jailer has tattoed his death club
on our heads and our blood
has flowed through rivers in one dream
together as we lay imprisoned in the streets
of the captor's city brain.

Please don't call me brother unless we have hunted
the miracle
slain the dragon
rolled through fields of clover dazed by the lights
of Venus calling our lust
kissing the angels of music.

Please don't call me brother unless we have ridden
the american highball
across the fantasy of Spring
ridden the stallions through the Winter's Sun
rode out
the redneck bars in Oklahoma City and Cheyenne.

Killed for our food in the mountains of Idaho
and fed the winos and over-the-hill hookers
on Two-bit Street in Ogden, Utah.

Pawned our jewelry and turquoise
for a Saturday night drunk and highjacked the comet
for a ten o'clock lay in Winnemuca.

Oh shit
for God's sake please don't call me brother
unless the water you have given me to drink
has been blessed by the Blue Herons of the Rainbow
flowing through the lands of my Grandmother
the Shoshone of the Snake River Plateau.
And the food you offer me has been cooked
by the wood fires of the Sun People
and blessed by the priests of the Moon Dance.

       Please call me brother
if you have hunted the grizzly
fished for the sturgeon below the falls
climbed Mount Shasta in the avalanche of Winter.

Call me brother
if we have kissed and crossed our blood wounds
in communion
in the ceremony of you and me
and the Sun as the eagle in the sky creation
and our children
the falcons
of this world this brotherhood

my brother.

DOVETAILING

We came through the sky
flying
as swift lovers of the sun
ageless in our journey
eclipsing the planets
as our wings caught the thermals
between vision and dreams.

We were ageless in our entrance —
as speed is lost in space
we were ancient
moving through each other a voice
carried by the wind.

We came into each a dreamer
as rivers rolled through our bodies
and we were at once
snow into oceans as one life
became our spines flying
from the beginning to the ancient
seventh sun of the highway God.

We came through
as earth leaves the fields into air
a spiral
into a multiple of dances
airborn
a double helix. We were forever a God.

We became through each other
the creation as flight becomes space
and space moves as solitude
of this earth lovers flying —
the forever moving wind.

TOUCHING

My parents were Mormons and gamblers
on the highball
through the lands of the Shoshone
and the leather plaited lasso of the one-ey'd cowpoke.

The geography is five thousand feet
high the winds
would never let you forget
that you had your soul backed
against the full house studpoker granite wall.

My eyes were searching constantly
for angels
and freighters
in the sagebrush, lipstick horizon.

Out there,
the snow was deeper than dreams,
and would bury the soft hips of women
in pick-ups and bullwhips.

Tough, you gotta be tough!

   OUT OF THE CHUTE. . .

riding a six legg'd Mustang
shooting fire
I would ride three beers drunk
rolling turquoise with one fantasy
touching Rodeo Gods with the other
laughing
at my broken hip
at the end of my deliverance.

Kill-a-deer,
skin out the soul of the Grizzly,
freeze my toes in the Winter of my thirteenth year,
get drunk
and ride the pick-up over forbidden snow passes
into Spring
defying Gods and Devils
falling drunk into the arena as a rodeo clown.

Fifteen years old,
a lilac Summer smoothed out the valley,
layed back into the sweetness of a woman's milk,
and I
went into the library and fought
with the witches and gargoyles
who guard the mysteries of Gods,
and I read my first book.

THE SONGS OF THE FLOWING RIVER

for
the Earth
Elia
and the Songs of the Flowing River

When the river is flowing it is all perfect
and I know exactly where I'll be in three million
years of praying into your eyes.

How high must I fly
to reach the journey of your dream?
I found a meadow
and centered my body surrounded by flowers
with a meadow lark as mantra
and the sky so full of you I was all alone inside of you
for the rest of my life.

As far as the sun is starborn
I can feel you with music in the rivers,
and in the trees, rain and mountains.
How many places you have touched with your beauty
I can only dream.

In the green spring of the changing forest
I begin to touch your wind in the evening sun.
And hear your voice as rainbow
moving my spirit into flight. I am airborn
oh spirit god flight lover.

Fly into this body
and we will sing the great creation of morning light
as lovers in the flowing river.

I feel everything
and all of the footprints that move life
as the circle.

Through flight there are no doors
to isolate the flowing river
that moves as dancers through my body.

I belong to everyone and everything,
and I am the sun and the summer storm.

If I sleep tonight inside your body
I will sing only the loveliest of songs.

I feel myself fly into the poppy fields
as color
I am so orange against the blue of the morning sky.

I would like to live with you forever
as a forest
lives with the pine, oak, and manzanita.

And deep into the center of the flowing river
the forest knows
that she is also a waterfall with green eyes
and
an owl.

Before I offer to you myself as seed to complete as magic
in silence of the hidden river which I am only half,
I will fast and walk the forest into mountains.

I will bathe in streams and waterfalls booming
from the sun-warmed snow until my body is spirit
in the pureness of attraction.

And then I will make a bed that holds all light
and wait for you to arrive as the dream told me how
you would appear as the new way into God.

I see you as the wind coming from the warmed island
of the secret sun leaving mountains
and moving spring into the forest,
and bringing with you a moon to hang in the sky.

And it will guide the night spirits into our bodies
as we become one with the flowing river.

Come into me O wind of the secret sun
as I am deep into the center of the fire. I am warm
and big and the bed is a circle of light.

I am dream into the center of the fire
come into me O wind of the sun
and we will fly through our bodies into the silence
as one dream a temple of beauty.

We are one
as a circle of flight O wind of the secret sun.

As my love for you becomes my body
the spirit that is eternal
leaves
and becomes the universe which is our space
to live as angels.

MAMA HERBS HOME MADE STEW

Deer tails,
apricot seeds, dark eyes and crystals.
Toe sucking
star gazing
nipple kissing
and the soul from the midnight turtle.

Golden seal
narrow gauge trains, sour-mash bourbon
and cocaine.

Columbian weed and Panama seeds
peyote feeds the stew . . .
How are you?
I am too, and I love you,
let's screw in the stew and cure the flu.

Turquoise and scarabs,
honey dew melons
Buddha bananas
and the first sperm of the honey bear.
Sweat from the horse's mane,
jonquils
and cocaine.

Once again . . .

Columbian weed and Panama seeds
peyote feeds the stew . . .
How are you?
I am too, and I love you,
let's screw in the stew and cure the flu
with
Mama Herbs Home Made Stew.

POTATOES AND ROSEHIPS

There are icicles hanging from my beard, and my belt is up two notches from the last hunt. My grandmother is blind, and keeps asking for some meat. She could live to be one hundred and twenty-five on potatoes and rosehips, and still have the sweetest smile in the valley. These are lean years to eat, but fat years to dream.

The arrows that I'm making will soon be ready. My bow is wrapped in deerskin tanned by my grandmother. Old skills that are necessary for the hunt. The smoothness of my walk, silence, and the beauty of being alone. One deer can replace a shopping mall she told me in her eighty-sixth year. These are lean years to eat, but fat years to dream.

You must be able to hunt alone, and with the silence of the falcon. Steal the wind and the colors of the sky, and walk without tracks. Bring home the meat, skin out the game, tan the hides, and prepare the meat for the smoker. You can write your sonnets later she would say, but first you must learn how to dream. With no meat in the pot your eyes will become walleyed. Here, take this scent and bring home our supper.

With my bow and arrows, my body covered with deerskin
rubbed with bay laurel, I move up the canyon. The wind is
blowing on my face, and I keep it there as a weather vane.
My grandmother is waiting. She has taught me everything,
except how to kill. She is hungry, and doesn't want to
live to be one hundred and twenty-five eating potatoes
and rosehips.

Go for the heart, I hear her voice as I pull back on
the string, finding the tension point where release is
lethal. The doe is round and beautiful, and I see my
grandmother as a young woman riding her buckskin through
the hills chasing butterflies and eagles. The doe looks
at me and I see my grandmother smile as I release the
arrow.

Sitting close to the fire we eat the meat in silence.
I rub her feet, trim the dry, hard skin from her bunions
with my hunting knife, and rub them with oil. She is
asleep, and only now can I return to my fantasies. Sit-
ting at my pine desk reading books of other worlds — of
poets who write like rainbows and rivers. Tomorrow we
will have a feast. We will dance and sing, and tell great
stories. And the next day I will take down my bow and
arrows, rub my body with mysteries, and move out alone
into the silence.

Bobbie Louise Hawkins

Old Security

When Sarah started college I started getting mail from insurance companies addressed to "Parents of Sarah Creeley." They were giving me options on Sarah's potential demise as if being a freshman meant life and death strikes again. The biggest graph of all.

Ten thousand dollars was the sum most often mentioned. Some kind of mystic choice masquerading as rational. Like a number that stands for infinity.

Old Security Life in Milwaukee, Wisconsin, enclosed a reply envelope addressed to their "Youth Marketing Division." Their letter starts "ACT NOW!"

True enough. Youth flies into the past even as we speak.

The letter says "Dear Parents: The dollar today does not buy what it bought yesterday."

It's like the math games section in Scientific American.

"The dollar today does not buy what it bought yesterday. However, our Life Insurance Policy is a product that yesterday's dollar can still buy."

That's for those of us who didn't spend yesterday's dollar the day before yesterday.

Under the heading of "Provisions" their ten thousand dollar policy is called "*Term* Life Insurance" up to the age of twenty-five. After the age of twenty-five it's called "*Permanent* Life Insurance". The main difference there is that *Term* costs you $24.00 a year but *Permanent* costs you $130. I think that's only fair. You get what you pay for. Apropos *Life*, Permanent has it all over Term.

"Even in an inflationary environment true values exist," is the way they put it.

Don't make the mistake of thinking that kind of

distinction doesn't count. Language can kill you. There's a linguist named Whorf who worked for Insurance Companies for awhile. His specialty was finding out where accidents were caused by language. For instance, he was called in on a job where a factory had had three explosions over a period of time, in the same place.

It seems that when the workers took breaks and smoked cigarettes out in the factory yard they all went to the left side of the yard. The right side was stacked with drums of industrial oil and there was a big sign that said "FULL." The workers were smart enough to not light up around all that oil. So they went to the other side where used drums were stacked under a big sign that said "EMPTY." The fact being the obvious one that the empties were full of gaseous vapors just waiting for a match.

Getting back to Old Security's *Facts to Consider.* The "proposed insured's future is Now!" Which sounds somehow like yesterday's dollar turned inside out. And the reason "Now" is so important is that Old Security is making life insurance (quote) "available to the proposed insured at an age when most can

qualify" (unquote). I guess that's a delicate way of saying that they're as far from dying as they'll ever be.

Those subliminal double plays are endless. One night Sarah and I were in the kitchen more or less watching a medical show on T.V. while I pasted up a collage on the kitchen table and she put together a circular jig-saw puzzle on a fold-out card table.

The plot ran like this:

A young woman who is going to be married goes to a surgeon to have a mole removed from her back because Bo deserves the best and when he gets her that's what he's going to get. The young woman's mother, a nervous, fashionable lady, comes with her because she and the surgeon are old friends and she wants him to remove the mole because Cissy deserves the best. . . etc. Cissy also needs the standard blood test and a general physical. During all that messing around the surgeon finds a lump in Cissy's breast which is cut into after a lot of by-play and it's malignant.

The big question at this point is how is Bo going to take to a one-breasted bride.

And he takes it badly. He goes out to walk around the block and think about it. Cissy is pondering keeping her breast by having massive X-Ray treatments. If she does it that way she runs a much higher risk of dying. They make it look like death is desirable alongside being sent back to the store.

"Have you ever seen *one* T.V. show where a *man* facing life and death got hooked on a cosmetic issue?" I ask Sarah.

"What do you mean 'cosmetic'?" she asked.

"Where the question of saving his looks was as important as saving his life."

"No, I never have," she said and got on with her jig-saw.

Bo decides to go with the loss and the plot moves into Phase Two.

Mama says she'll only feel secure if her old friend does the knife work.

Enter a young surgeon who has done a heart transplant on the old surgeon.

"Your heart won't stand it," he says. "I won't let you take the risk."

It all starts to function like a variation on that nursery rhyme where the old woman is trying to get her pig over the stile.

The mother is persuaded to use somebody else.

The operation is successful.

Cissy is provided with a duplicate in rubber.

The happy ending is the young surgeon and the old surgeon walking into the sunset down a hospital corridor, both hearts beating a regulation number of beats per minute.

"Huh!" I grunt. "They just mean to ignore the percentages."

"You mean all those heart transplant people have died?" Sarah asked, looking shocked.

"Honey," says I, "it's even worse than that. All the people who don't have heart transplants die too."

But back to Old Security. They have a P.S. on their letter about "the advantages of independent decision, without pressure, made in private."

Well, I'll buy that.

Pitches and Catches

There's a gap in the greater American consciousness about the low-downest level of the magazine business and I'm going to feed a little into it out of my own true-life experience.

I answered an ad when I was seventeen that invited young women to travel in a chaperoned group and earn while you learn. For me the real hook was New Orleans. They were enroute to New Orleans, learning and earning.

I've always wanted to see New Orleans (and I still haven't. This isn't a story with a reasonable progression and an appropriate ending. It's just one more instance of "Oh, see what fits our foolish hopes.").

I telephoned and made an appointment to be interviewed at the Kiva Motel on Central Avenue in Albuquerque, New Mexico. I got the job. I can't imagine what might have disqualified me.

The job was selling magazine subscriptions door-to-door. That was how you earned and the learning part had to do with the underlying principles of salesmanship. Within that simple and usual projection there were nuances so abstract that they could only be the outcome of bureaucratic thought, an inherent growth principle of crummy thinking. For instance, one word you never say if you're a magazine salesman is "magazine." Pros peddle "books."

When the lady of the house, that entrenched functionary, opens the door and looks at you and says "I don't want any magazines" what you really start to work on is that piece of semantics.

We were handling Better Homes and Gardens books, Good Housekeeping books, McCalls books, Saturday Evening Post books; I mean there was just no way in the world to get around it that what we were doing was peddling magazines.

And all we had to come against truth with, our naked faces looking able and our bodies on the line, our only tool against those hostile faces in that knowing world was our "pitch".

We memorized the "pitch" word for word. It was awful, just on the edge of literate with total non-sequitors that had to be carried on pure voice alone, the eyes blank as if nothing had just gone screwy in the non-context.

I wish I remembered the damned thing. I'd give you the highlights. It was so eminently forgettable. In fact, that was a problem at the time. Every morning we congregated in one of the motel rooms and practiced the pitch. It was so much an applied piece of goods. Take away the screen door and the lady of the house, and the mind goes blank. The pitch disperses like gas, like any elective fantasy. So we practiced it daily, to remember it, to put it into the day like substance. Then we went for breakfast. Then we were driven to the "territory" and let out with our kits.

Well, I'll start at the beginning.

One morning early three new Mercurys stopped in front of our house on Byers Avenue and I came out with my mother's Samsonite suitcase. It and me were stashed into one of the cars and we headed for Arizona.

I was given a copy of the pitch and suffered the really expectable failing of seeing where it could be improved. It was like coming up against steel. The pitch was not to be improved. The pitch was absolute. Questioning the pitch wasn't a question at all.

"It works," the lady who had interviewed me said. "We've got experts who don't do anything but come up with the perfect pitch that works and this is it."

I started my training. I memorized the pitch. I went with the top peddler and saw how it steamrolled through objections. There were places that were pauses to let the "prospect" speak. According to the objection made, you responded. And the only point of that little interchange was to get rid of the mounting tension that wanted to resist your salesmanship. The words it all took meant nothing.

It hurt me to see how the prospects went under. I didn't at all take it as a triumph. And in my heart of hearts I resolved that when they turned me loose I wasn't going to use the pitch.

I thought there must be a human place where I could stand and leave the person of the prospect unravaged. I believed that there were people who actually wanted to have subscriptions to magazines. And it was true that the rates we offered were the lowest going. I figured that with whole towns turning over under our crew I could depend on ratios.

That's how I learned at the age of seventeen that you can't underestimate human nature.

Straightforward and barefaced I would start to outline the magazine subscriptions I had to sell.

I didn't achieve any one-to-one relationships. What

I did was I gave a lot of housewives the opportunity for long overdue revenge.

You know the kind of expression you see on the faces of satisfied lynch mobs who mean to have their picnic now that the action's over? That's the look that followed me away down the sidewalk.

I was a magazine salesman who handed my body over. Boy, was I soft.

So then I started hating them, sitting smug, and me on my way back to the crew to hold down low man on the totem pole.

I started using the pitch. And it worked. I got a reputation among our little group.

It looked like I'd make a book salesman.

What I couldn't bypass was the moral torque. I was into an increasing anxiety. I was a hotshot acceptable criminal and the vanishing return on it was how I was tucking away subliminal guilt into bits of myself where I didn't have to pay attention. There was an accruing factor that earning money didn't touch.

We got to south Texas, still enroute to New Orleans.

One morning our boss gave us a pitch of her own on the value of poverty.

me standing in the swirl
of its dust.

I sloped off across a sandy
lot to a shed standing by
itself in the blistering sun.
It was the kind of arrange-
ment where the top half of
the front raised on hinges
and stayed up with a stick,
opening the place into a
counter.

There was a stool and an
old kitchen chair standing
on the ground in front and
I sat there all afternoon
with an oldish mexican
woman, drinking coke and
learning spanish.

"Hello."

"How are you?"

"Good morning."

"Good afternoon."

"Good evening."

I spent that hot afternoon
rejoining the human race
just outside of Houston.

We were supposed to have
a treat that night. The
Director for that area was
going to take us to dinner
at the Emerald Room in
the Shamrock Hotel. We
were going to hear somebody
named Brandywine play for
a singer named Dorothy
Shay. She was billed as the
"Park Avenue Hillbilly."

I missed that reward,
spent the evening packing
and feeling alone and floppy.
The bird had split the cage.

I didn't feel noble or even
relieved. I just felt undefined.

I was really young, but
of course I didn't know it
then.

The sense of it was that
poor people are pushovers.
They don't have muscles.

"Don't let the territory
mislead you," she said. "I've
had some of my best days
in territory just like this."

Because I was still new
and it was another moral
jog to be gained they sent
me along with someone
more experienced and I
watched her talk a thin,
ruined woman in a shanty
into three subscriptions,
complete with the first
payment. The woman took
three dollars out of a coffee
can where they didn't have
much company.

They put me out on a
dirt road and the Mercury
went flashing away leaving

Jonathan London

VIVALDI

twisted ferns   monkey fists   dripping moss

furlings and
unfurlings

flutes with flamingo wings
fly thru us

pull the fists from our throats
with their song

LOW DARK LIGHT RISING HIGH
                    for Stephanie Mines

excuse me there you
you with the venturesome smile you
you with the Oriental Jewish Gypsy eyes
cats eyes   hungry eyes   giving eyes
teeth a flash of Kali
body a marvelous maya invention
Mother   Mother   Mother
woman
giving birth to
self   to selves   to Self
to all the dimensions of all
your dreams to all the dimensions of all
          excuse me
that i betray your size
by my littleness
and yet and·yet
grow enormous with inhalation
of your
          light

POINT REYES
          for Maureen

sharp spires of green grass
beneath
white fallow deer

we eat our basket
full of goodies

we get drunk
on the beach

we get drunk
on each other

the surf
spreads foam lips

about the cuffs
of our fleeing pants

we are kissed

the sun is in its sky

we are on the Earth

there's a fire that warms us
it comes of   proximity

curled in the
wind's uneasy harness

we have this   and this   and this

GREEK LIGHT, BLUE VISION
for Kendall

Greek light, blue vision
sky of imminent emersion
philosophies dubbed
by Zorba's dance
we crush the grapes
drink the wine
and dance and dance
and together rise
full with love
large with wonder
light with light
arm in arm

THERE IS SUCH A TIME AS NOW

there is such a time as now
sun soothing the tightened flesh
cup rising tilting spilling coffee
hotly down
                        the chair tilting
leaning on the weathered wood
of your back porch, with you in it
inhaling soft air
                        warm
the tomato plant by your head
pushing yellow flowers
and pungent, musky, earth
                        smell
            yes
and pulleys squealing up the rickety stairs
where the neighbor lady hangs her laundry
though there's barely breeze to swing the
                        eucalyptus leaves
in the next yard, but
just enough
                gently

METAMORPHOSIS
for Nancy

the tree i stood upon
became
a pillar of water
a limb
rushed thru my hand
sending cold branches
thru my chest
down thru my ribs
down thru my legs
my roots gripped
the vanishing soil
my leaves trembled
and clawed at my limbs
and when all was washed
away
i was a tree torn bare
but for the sky
which hung from my limbs
like skin   and the sun
which became an owl
and sat on a limb
and winked and cooed
and became the moon

Joanne Kyger

UP MY COAST
Stories of the Hookooeko
from C. Hart Merriam

1

First, there were the First People.
And the first people changed
into trees, plants, rocks, stars, rain, hail and
Animals.
And then Animals made our People.

LIGHT comes from SUN WOMAN. Whose body
is covered
with shining Abalone Shells.

She came across the Pacific
on a raft.
So did Coyote. Sun Woman kept on going.
Come back! Coyote sent some people to get

her back. She wouldn't come back. So
Coyote sent enough men to bring her back
whether she wanted to or not.

They tied her in ropes
and brought her back
to make light for her people. She was so bright
it was hard to look at her.

2

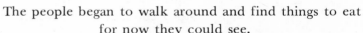

The people began to walk around and find things to eat
for now they could see.

3

Moon Man, Coyote Man, and Lizard Man made the People.
They argued a lot.
Moon Man gave people his head
but Coyote Man said he should have paws, just like him.

          But how can he take *hold* of things
said Lizard Man,
        thankfully winning his point,
              and gave us
five fingers, just like his own.
          Coyote was pissed
and he's still hunting the lizard.

4

When the first person died, Lizard Man felt real bad
and set to work to bring him back to life.
           But Meadow Lark came
                  and drove him away saying

People no good, People smell.
             When they die, they better stay dead.

5

Robin brought the fire. He traveled
a long way to get it,
            and every night on the way back
he lay with his breast on it,
            to keep it warm.
It turned his breast red.
           He gave fire to the people
and put some
       into the Buckeye tree
     so they could get it whenever they needed it.
Just rub
     the Buckeye stick against
            a dry wood stick,
   this makes the flame come out.
   Humming Bird brought the fire too
   just look under his chin.

6

Coyote was sitting on top of Sonoma Peak
and the earth was all covered with water.
He got there from across the ocean
                on his raft of tules and split sticks.
A feather comes floating up from the west too.
HI! Who are You?
                        And the feather doesn't answer.
            So, Coyote tells him all about his families and friends
        and What's Happening!
                            And the feather leaps up and says
I'M FALCON! Your grandson! Wow!
                        So they talk
every day
                and after a while Coyote Man notices FROG WOMAN
        always just jumping out of hand.
                                But the water
started to go down after four days and it took her longer
            to leap to the water so
                        Coyote Man caught her.
                                            And
when he caught her, Imagine his surprise!
                                She was his own wife!
            from over the ocean! Small World!
Then Coyote Man
                took a bunch of feathers of different kinds
to the top of Sonoma Peak   And Threw them
        into the air
                    and the wind carried them off
    and scattered them around
    and the next day there were people
                All Over the Land.

7

Coyote Man brought the   *big clam*
                              to make shell money
and planted it at Bodega Bay.
                              This is the place

          and the only place
          where the *big clam*
                    was in the beginning.
Where ever else you find it now,
                    the seed came from here.
     The Tomales Bay people
                    got their seed from here.

8

Meadow Lark Man can be a pain in the ass.
                              He already said people
          couldn't come to life again on the third or fourth day, and
he talks too much and gossips
                    and says awful things to the People.
He says, I know what you're up to, you're really stingy,
          you're only dark on the outside.
                    Under your skin
          you're as white and mean as a white man.

9

When People die their ghost crosses the ocean

over the path of the wind

to the Village of the dead.   Sometimes

they come back and dance in the roundhouse.
You can't see them

But you can hear them.

Robert Bly

VERSIONS OF KABIR

How Restless Kabir Is

My body and my mind are in depression
            because you are not with me.
How much I love you and want you in my house!
When I hear people describe me as your bride
            I look sideways ashamed,
because I know that far inside us we have never met.
Then what is this love of mine?
I don't really care about food, I don't care about sleep,
I am restless indoors and outdoors.
The bride wants her lover as much
      as a thirsty man wants water.
And how will I find someone who'll take a message
            to the Guest from me?
How restless Kabir is all the time! How much he wants to see the Guest!

The Ruby

The small ruby everyone wants has fallen out on the road.
Some think it is east of us, others west of us.

Some say, "among primitive earth rocks," others "in the deep waters."

Kabir's instinct told him it was inside,
      and what it was worth,
and he wrapped it up carefully in his heart cloth.

The Flute

The flute of interior time is played whether we hear it or not.
What we mean by "love" is its sound coming in.
When love hits the farthest edge of excess, it reaches wisdom.
And the fragrance of that knowledge!
It penetrates our thick bodies,
it goes through walls —
Its network of notes has a structure as if a million suns
      were arranged inside.
This tune has truth in it. Where else have you heard a sound like this?

Inside this clay jug there are canyons and pine mountains,
     and the maker of canyons and mountains!
All seven oceans are inside, and hundreds of millions of stars.
The acid that tests gold is there, and the one who judges jewels.
And the music from the strings no one touches, and
     the source of all water.

If you want the truth, I will tell you the truth:
Friend, listen: the God whom I love is inside.

Shall I flail with words, when love has made the space
    inside me full of light?
I know the diamond is wrapped in this cloth, so why
    should I open it all the time and look?
When the pan was empty, it flew up; now that
    it's full, why bother weighing it?

The swan has flown to the mountain lake!
Why bother with ditches and holes any more?
The Holy One lives inside you —
why open your other eyes at all?

Kabir will tell you the truth: Listen, brother!
The Guest, who makes my eyes so bright,
has made love with me.

I don't know what sort of a God we have been talking about.

The caller calls in a loud voice to the Holy One at dusk.
Why? Surely the Holy One is not deaf.
He hears the delicate anklets that ring on the feet of an insect
        as it walks.

Go over and over your beads, paint designs
        on your forehead,
wear your hair matted, long, and ostentatious,
but when deep inside you there is a loaded gun,
        how can you have God?

I said to the wanting-creature inside me:
What is this river you want to cross?
There are no travelers on the river-road,
and no road.
Do you see anyone moving about on that bank, or resting?
There is no river at all, and no boat, and no boatman.
There is no towrope either, and no one to pull it.
There is no ground, no sky, no time, no bank, no ford!

And there is no body, and no mind!
Do you believe there is some place that will make the soul
        less thirsty?
In that great absence you will find nothing.

Be strong then, and enter into your own body;
there you have a solid place for your feet.
Think about it carefully!
Don't go off somewhere else!

Kabir says this: just throw away all thoughts
        of imaginary things,
and stand firm in that which you are.

Pat Urioste

A SONG FOR BRENDA

The review comes from California,
has his name there in passing
mention of words he's published
in New York.

I stare at it a long time.
I never knew him. You unfolded
old copies of his poems
in Colorado like kaleidoscopes
so I could see how fine
you thought them.

You were a wispy reed. Wind
sang lullabies in your hair.
All that year in rooms of incense
and posters we were chairless, drew
chords with crayons on the floor.

Your old Haight-Ashbury lover
chanted in the door one day
and I could see you were going
when the air burst into sparks
around the edges of your movements.

I tied up the words you gave — his,
yours — what I had left of you.
Your California dreamer opened
his wrists later
and then you were alone.

You never sent more of your poet's
poems. My letters wafted
down some San Francisco well.

His name says he's alive and writing:
bad connection, but nonetheless
a thread which has gone on
spinning past pain, making me
hear that somewhere a soughing wind
still makes music of your hair.

WHAT I WANT YOU CAN'T GIVE ME

what i want you can't give me
what i want i'll never have
dedicated to self-denial and abasement
my horoscope says
who would have dreamed it in the orange groves
during lightless nights when the peacocks
cried from spanish tile rooftops?
who would have guessed how closely
my awareness would crest upon the rim
of tomorrow's changes?
how far behind i'd leave niggertown guilts
and tropical humidity?

even if you love me more than any other
with your indian passion
you can't give me what i want
but this time i understood that
when we met
and it's alright now
in the mountains after a cold rain
with a starful of sky and dripping tall pines
silvery shimmering aspens
in the mountains
where i walk alone
who would have thought it on the beach?
during the sunrises of palm and hibiscus
over the lavender edge of ocean?
that my words would want me
to walk with someone
who'd allow/force me
to walk alone.

UPON BEING EVICTED

It is not this room we will miss
but the lying on decked amber
with daylight dying through
a wide wavering sweep of window
washed with rustling leaves
so thick, so green.

Organ and guitar
shiver into the dimming spaces
with vibrations that climb
the cream water-crinkled sides.

The dark-tressed mermaid
couches her sucked-in curves
across the mossy bow
with her large blue stare
sounding
the rippling grasses below.

Children run there
with no noise rising through
this organ's moaning pulse.
Their hair floats up and down
their arms rise and fall
and their bodies leapfrog
through billowing grass
to the pitch
of our high-masted music.

Blue-tressed silver fish
and green-locked nymph
turn back up to the skies
shimmering through a tossing
chartreuse surface
and sigh:

It is not the vaulted thrust
of this rounded prow
we will go green after
but the lying beside phosphorous
with all swirling insides
flown out vacant eyes
tacking fix by slow fix
up the rippling leaves of glass.

Dale Samoker

Ray Cosseboom

SOME KIND OF BIRD

"Some sea birds have the colors of tunics, you know," This New
Woman said, "bare napkins in the sky. A whole village all in
flock," and laughed, — and there we were in miles of blueberries,
Cape St. Francis ripe in the wind, — and as we ran we drifted, —
clouds going by so fast they bobbed with the sea ducks, — and
once near some large waves pounding on the rocks, the spray that
filled the air colored rainbow our view, and we saw three ships
in the distance, icebergs navigating passed seals, cliffs hovering.
  "If you grow up in Newfoundland you learn to float early," This
New Woman smiled again, — and then Bell Island shifted a little, —
had ferries full of school-going children, — and dark black cormorants
rode the currents, — teachers of shadows swaying with goldenrods, —
snowstorms so deep the lights went out, — and up wood walks ptarmigans
fluttered, Pete's dory, abandoned cottages.
  And all that year wherever we rowed small islands surfaced, decks
with icebergs, July with a storm flag, Signal Hill, a Russian fleet.
  "Some good, this island," This New Woman once said to me, "to
live here you have to be some kind of bird," and smiled.

THE LANGUAGE THE WILDFLOWERS USED

Riding in New Hampshire. A mushroom colored sky. Your scarf growing
among the aspens, a bridge blurred in a silhouette, a splashed sun. You
said, "The hike we are now on is the same one the foliage is taking."
  Then the splash re-occurs. It kisses a small opening deep in the woods
evaporizing. Far away a farm is now long. In your eyes the language the
wildflowers used goes deep, a well built rock fence you
  undress on, and sat like a vision New Hampshire keeps having every
October in blurs continuously more fused. "I want to be satisfied by an
apple tree," you said.
  I splash. The aspens. The fading farm. Then when you touch me I begin
to grow: "There are deep places in the woods like this one," you said,
"that I live in year around."

CLIMBING

In those days logging trucks jammed the air with their
sounds, red tailed hawks kept giving their shadows away, and
at night, coyote howls came down Grizzly Mountain, and stopped
near an old gray mailbox.

And Joyce and I were climbing up to the forks of Neil
Creek that day, the chirps the dream the birds were in was
five a.m., and the cool air found in a canyon a trail beyond
this dream: this climb.

When Joyce and I got to Phantom Orchid Ridge, we watched
the sunlight slowly peeking over the mountains: splashing in
its blossoms. Water-ouzels flew in and out of our conversations.
Trout had shadows in their darts.

Then they flew away — these shadows — and at noon reappeared
again high up in some meadows. And as Joyce was lying down near
some cattails with a piece of grass in her mouth, she laughed
and said, "It's kind of funny, but we are always climbing towards
what is flowing to us."

A BIRD

As Joyce was showing me her art she kept leaning against
an easel, and when she left I saw a seagull flying over an elm
tree.

Some thoughts lean art in the wrong direction, but Joyce
is just the opposite: she seems to have discovered a new kind
of bird in what she is willing to show.

And as I continued to walk, I started letting my thought
show me what it was carrying, and when I'd done this a bird
appeared in my thinking:

And suddenly I realized that I hadn't left what Joyce had
been showing me, but was carrying around the same

Direction, the kind that shows you so much, at the end of
everything I write some bird escapes, and you are left leaning
on what it all means.

LIQUEFIED

The sea today is waving goldenrods in its splashes, pollen of
tuna, somersaulting cottages. Old cliffs are turning to seed.

Then the tide comes in stronger, the spray has sunrays in it,
blueberries in currents, someone's wharf. An island just took off
with the gulls.

I stand here: liquefied, and feel the ports my nerves are on,
the trolling sounds of bells being washed further and further
inward, are the tangled heaves of an everchanging dream —

and as I begin to swim in it, I reclaim the original thought
I had: there can never be a shore that's mine.

SHADOWS OF A LARGER HAND

Down the Rogue River in Oregon I put my hand underwater,
and there in a large blue heron shadow four fingers and a thumb
took place. And it flew past, unconnected from the rest of me,
and landed a few feet near a large dark rock.

Sunlight had come with no body, and where my hand used to
be, my thought became. I was flowing in that river. The wind
stirred. Some voices that were hard to hear were in the shadows.
Their meanings

Went by in a canoe. And when a raccoon came out of hiding,
and crawled near the river, every voice I ever heard came back.
I saw shadows of a larger Hand.

EVERY TIME WE SPOKE

Every time we spoke that early Thanksgiving morning in
North Hampton, Massachusetts, our breath frosted the air,
Autumn leaves fell, and as you were standing on a large rock,
the mist over the hill in a little field behind you dept rising.
There was dew in our laughs, a red tailed hawk circling.

And when we got back to your grandfather's house, we ate
our oatmeal, flipping through scrapbooks, the sunlight from
a large window, your mother saying, "What did you see on your
walk?"

And you sketched a little picture for me, and wrote a note
under it saying, "There is nothing so small, but my tenderness
can paint it large in a background of gold."

LET IT FLAP

The sea today is taking off its clothes. A flag is flapping
up your sleeve, and gray clouds go by your collar. You're as
lovely as a whitecap set out of doors to play for the first time.
Your dark colored hair is the foam sails tip in. Up your legs a
tanker is coming in.

I'm going to take your flag and use it for my own. In the
distance, shouts of children think the inner tube that just blew
in is the one they lost. What they are losing are whitecaps day
by day. There are schools in this wind, tearing loose. I think
your body needs a sail, and as I take your sweater off you, let
it flap.

Dear, April is the name of fun. My tide sucks you in all at
once. A gull there is unbuttoned white in the wind. Name it,
and we will find the sea a roar every touch we do.

GREATER THINGS HAPPENING

We were in Medicine Hat National Park in Wyoming, lightning
crashing in the distance, a sunset near us in pink, large rocks
casting shadows. And Joyce ran out of the car and said excitingly,
"Forget the tent and the campfire now, there are greater things
happening," — and grabbed my hand and continued to run.

And when we got to a small hill, we sat down on it, and
suddenly we saw a black heron sitting on a rock in the middle
of a stream — lightning splashing in its feathers — large clouds
heading North, cattle grazing.

And we laid down on that hill for hours until the storm
ceased, the stars came out, and the wind was whispering through
a small pine. Our kisses had manzanita bushes in them, glimmering
grass, syllables blossoming.

And after we had set up our tent, built a campfire, and
were in our sleeping bags, faint coyote sounds joined the
snaps in the ashes the logs were making,

And there was one minimum that night:
a lake leaping in its arcs, silt like silver when Joyce said,
"It sure is good to be here."

AFTER THE STORM

After the storm we shoveled out. Icicles had grown over night.
The frost designs on the windows helped get our car started. Children
had sleds and skates in their dreams.

Inside of me a taxi got stuck. Things I hadn't thought of for
a long time kept asking for a shovel. The designs there had you in it.
The hills were steep.

And then you fell asleep and understood this white dream better.
There on that bed taxis came and went designed in your mind. Icicles
kept children from being thirsty. And you slept for days, dream
after dream being shoveled out, until finally you realized it was
time for the snowplow: you pulled your blankets close to you, you
got ready in drifts.

And suddenly you woke up:
a part of your dream had collected on the evergreen branches during
the night, the sun was shining, and you knew you had dreamed a
storm into happening.

The first thing you did was get the snowplow out of your
thinking, and tossed the white blankets off you and begin to move.
You got dressed in what you expected.

And that is actually where the dream continued. You realized
taxis work in storms there. Your life was whiter than you had
supposed.

But you really were not awake. The storm for you was stuck
inside of you. Everything you did became the shovel. The icicles
just hung there, slowly dripping. Days skied past you. Events had
rudders on them. Voices made drifts. All of this was inside of
you and it was one color: white: a storm.

And it snowed and it snowed. In your bedroom people started
waiting for that taxi to get dug out. The pillow wore a hood to
keep warm. Your tears were attached to your roof as icicles. Your
story snored.

Christine Zawadiwsky

THE BLACK ORCHIDS

Four doors mark the corners of these halls
and in each doorway there lies a flower.
The flowers are resting, the flowers are sleeping,
all except the orchid that's been known to supply
romance at every hour and for any good reason.

One would say its petals ring with fresh blood.
One would say its eyes are nothing but black holes.
But I'll swallow freedom and leave death near
the doorway. And I'll tilt its head like a
child, toward the sky.

Four boxes are singing with protection
and reason. And these are not the boxes
in which the black orchids lie. Their corpses
are as beautiful as any rainy season, their damp
tongues have been known to kiss lost virgins good-bye.

A SOLID GOLD HAT

I was on the sun. I wanted to bring part of it
back for you. The Sun God was bursting, his
silver stallion trampling the eggs that fell
from the nest of a songbird. I was on the moon.
It was glorious, silver! Filled with blue eggs
and mysterious holes. It was open, open, open.
Open skies, open fields. An open back door
where the wasps flew in and pierced the afternoon
with their song.

We fell towards sleep. I tried to fall alone.
You had been throwing darts at a blindfold.
I had been following the great magician
who travels across the face of the country healing,
soothing, filling his hat up with songs, nodding
his head towards rebirth and salvation. I had first
disappeared on the day spring was born.

Crossfires! Crossfires! And strange fears
and loathings. I'm sure to be riding
the golden stallion, I'm sure not to die
in the afternoon. Dying does not make a person
thirsty: loving leaves you dry, though
I longed to be born the first time you sighed,
the first time they carried your joys to the moon.

CLOSE YOURSELF AROUND ME, LOVE

Let me close into myself like a fist,
like a person falling out of another's love,
the way the human heart is wedged into the body,
crushed and on its side, nothing like its symbol.
Let me be the lit window,
the unerring eye,
with a woman to visit me every hour
bearing gifts of sweets and consolation,
her heart open like a wound.
Let me receive you as more than my own.
Let me take you in as more than my life's sorrow.
Help me to pivot the reasoning part of the brain
and to remember my love as a cut-apart orange,
each section more bitter than the one I've eaten.
Then I'll bypass those persons I love more often
and imagine that with each coming day I'll be free
to cut down new cherries and to cry with the willows
and to drain with a sieve the open-ended sky.

BLACK OLIVES

Black olives, black olives,
how I love your shiny skins;
the salty taste as
I break your meat open!
Here is what I am most capable
of doing:
being attracted to the only man in the room
who is suicidal.
His skin is like yours, sleek and beautiful,
and dark because it reflects the world.

Black olives, I have eaten you
in places of affliction;
while giving birth to a man's father;
and when my tooth was cutting through
the surface of my childhood.
I couldn't have lived without you!
The sting of bright foods
would have riddled my tongue.

Why couldn't I have married you,
Black Olives?
You would have waited for me like
a man outside my window
strapped to a ladder,
a dark hammer at his elbow.

Odds plus odds make evens.
But today I've eaten three black olives;
one for me,
one for me,
and one just for you.

Adrian Brooks

THE WOOLSEY SUITE
for Peter and Julia

In your house where I have come
time and time and time again
weary with my wandering and weary
with the world, I sleep where I am
no more the Stranger just in
from somewhere down the road.

In your good house of fires and wines
and nights prolonged to the latest
possible hour (with tomorrow
another work day for you, of course
for me), a precious glimpse of a life
line, a life abandoned in my fantasy
of artistic global "conquest."

Perhaps, in the end, we are all fools.

But on your hill overlooking forest
and faraway bay where the moon rises
above the waves and smoke blows
across First Valley to the mesa
I am another task attended to
needs appeased, sheltered, loved and
tucked into a cosy bed, to sleep
to quiet morning.

In your house I am the odd one out/in
for this time being/human/in love
you give which cannot be repeated.

In your house with open shelves
and flowers at your windows
I am the stranger
perched on a kitchen stool
sipping soup or tea or hot mulled wine
before the wood burning stove.
Thick with sweaters and tuned to tales
of horses pulling up lame or rare
mushrooms discovered high on the ridge
collected and prepared for supper.

In your house where families reunite
I am the ghost come by to drink
more than cool white wine.

Will it be summer, then, with Julia
hair tied back with ribbons and proud
of how Peter does with his Arabian mare?
Will it be another feast of salmon
cucumber and chablis?
Will it be winter with wet sheepdog
mournful at the door or the warm
burn of marijuana?

JULIA AND PETER   INVERNESS· CALIFORNIA   1975

Lovers and friends/growing as we do
each to each over years through differences.
From summer slow suntanned days
of first beginning.
From long distance letters ending
"Come home soon. We love you."
From trunks in storage and sound of rain
on rhodedendron — smacking the leaves
on otherwise dismal autumn evenings.
From nights where the fire burned low
or endlessly wicked village scandals
involving married men.
From all these weekends, months, episodes
over years all leading to your door
and this poem for you, for you . . .
Julia . . . Peter

                    *

Dark trees just after dawn
leaves the sky almost white
or washed of color, blanched
unable to pierce the scar
webbing of black branches.

These trees — launching up
steep slopes of First Valley
known by no other name.
These trees — dark with damp
smell of damp ground.
Unyielding secret kept
between the bay and sea.

                    *

. . . and yes, when you say you want it
or need it too, I agree and bend
with you all willows — overladen
with tears with rain with river
music in the drift, the drift
the dances we do to keep the ghosts
appeased (for they *are* fearsome).

And when you all beauty in your way
bend with me in my passionate bed
of tender ache and sorrow — I float
over river flowing out to open sea
calling, "Take me with you as you go
but do not wander far!"

The moment capsizes.
The dream changes.
The dreamer sleeps on.
(No one knows the difference).

Fantasy remains in the quiet
of untouched pine. It is a dream
in blue, charcoal grey and white
but at the sides, as encroaching
suburbs — Day bares those fatal teeth
and plays the trump
so called "reality."

                    *

Back to the same village.
Back to the lanterns
beside white camellia and bay.
Back to bishop pine and madrone
and soft wind moaning over the mesa
down to Tomales Bay.
Back to this world I have known
and loved and love again.
Back to dusty roads snaking overgrown
ravines and dark green canyons
yellowing afternoon July.
Back to the same town
of open doors
of wine at table
of wood smoking the night sky.

Over and over I call the name
remember the place and recite
the wisdom of friends and former loves.
Over and over again I remember
beaches known year after year —
the ride to certain valleys
as families change their worries.
Over and over again I return
hitching into town
with my secret inventory.
(Now I don't explain).

But again and always
with the same friends
in the early afternoon
tapestry of leaves
and white wooden trellis
we who survive
consider the middle way.

Is it only age?

. . . coffee not quite as warm
as years before or faces
slightly less tanned.

Can this be the passing of years —
invisible answers in a tangible wind?

I have come home to California
to floral walls fading in wood frame
houses. Cotton in prints and patterns.
And this time, the kisses promising
no spring
but one full moment of relief
in the arms of a friend.
Less fire, perhaps, longer
breaths as we say similar words
with a difference.

I have come home to California
the only place I truly move
to bury my porcelain masks
in stately ghost dances.

John Read

In a swirl of
      clear
           water
   Golden Carp.

Let them swim!

JUST SITTING

How much incense before this
stops?
No waste, no bells, no paper
poems.
Blue and silver tuna thoughts
(never mind no thinking)
jump right in/write all this down
remember tuna/the word
how much more sitting?

no waiting/jump right in

to breathing
mudra fingers
just
touch
eyes lift floor
floor and chin
equal
spine/occiput/ass a massive
pyramid
support sky, support candle, floor, legs
take them all together for
nothing but me
me, nothing.
Even fish swim here
no waiting at all
huge empty filled to the top
jump right in.

Thinking just like
eyelids/identical composition
transparent/deep
blue and silver tuna

Michael Sykes

FOUR SONNETS

I'd rather be doomed to leave
than not be dreamed at all, if all
the commonplace, the new unique, or if
the world were gone or never, be
a light, a loveliness, allure,
could spell my dance, my green
awakening into East, the opening,
across the sun down to the West,
behind the mountains, swallowed by earth,
I could turn, and trembling in the dark
thunder beneath the sea, feel the faint
beginnings, stir the unborn mind, begin
a gathering, from clouds of dust
to star, afar within, again ago.

I have come by way of noon
sidelong, slipping into afternoon
bone lazy, flesh bearing
a whimsical, a Cheshire grin
into again, begin with you
your milk loveliness against the rain
I lose you, I find you, again
against the sky, faced with love
with iris, magnolia trace, of
you in you in me I find you
beneath the leaves, from out my sleeve
you drift are dreaming me, under the tree
trembling, tunes sifting from my skin
alive again, a grin, of you and you and me.

Reunions of birds remind me of death,
sprung from the reiteration of Spring
like blubs of light blown through space;
the overture of water falling through ravines
recalls the dry revelation of stone,
the barren fields beneath a previous sun.
It all falls endlessly to change,
the Great Imposter with his bag of tricks
posing through the intricacies of time.
He takes me by the hand, the old buffoon;
his smile a gift of yesterdays, of life,
winning me over with his charm,
while underneath the ageless beauty of his skin
the hard teeth of his skeleton lie exposed.

Old bowls believe the emptiness of form
and empty shelves have voices of their own
galaxies collide without a sound
while in the silent furnace of the universe
a furrowing is found within a womb
among the willows and the river
runs a breath of spring invisible
as whistling from another room
reminds the bird below the earth to fly
and flung among the flowers and the wheels
our bodies reel a single song to spring

all tidings told all merciful our father king
our mother hold our dreams unfold
in all ways we ourselves we are discovering

A FLY BUZZED BY ME WHILE I SLEPT

A fly buzzed by me while I slept
and tore my jerkin loose;
a girl sat by my side and wept,
and stroked her long-necked goose.

The sun half-hidden drew the day
from dawn to early dusk;
while in the cloister where I lay:
an odor thick with musk.

When darkness came my eyes were wide,
my hands and feet were cold,
and when I turned into my bride
this dream to me she told:

You dreamt of water far and deep,
you walked upon the shore,
and from the belly of your sleep
you drew an oaken oar;

and setting out upon the waves
your oar became a snake,
and sought the shadows in the caves
which lay beneath the lake.

The night before me drew me forth,
I walked among the trees;
a star flew swiftly to the north
and brought me to my knees.

The world below was turned to gold,
the heavens filled with light,
and life was more than I could hold,
and death returned to life.

ADVICE TO THE LOVELORN

I grumble near the bottom of 32,
                              mind askew,
     all experience a footnote to my life,
                              a wife
and children, happy home, a broken home,
                    I chew on bones,
          lingering over the feast,
                              the least
I can do is clear the table, sweep the floor,
                              the more
     I eat the heavier on my feet,
                    I grow to know,
          and what's the use?
                    abuse?
          I clutch defeat
and flirt ambition to succeed;
                    the greed of gain
dancing on the skulltop of my mood,
                              I brood
          beneath my dreams in opposition to myself,
                              the elf,
          the flickering protean pan-man that is me,
                              I see
the field above the coast, the Host of seasons
          propped against the clouds, the leisurely sky
     alive with blue betweenwhiles
                              whistling
                    birds and starlight
          on the rooftop of my life
                    my life!
Why be dark and broken in the basement
     huddling in a janitorial consciousness,
          deliberate
in a stained and rumpled overcoat,
          the calendars of my dream vacations
     peeling on the wall?
                    It's all
a drift of self-deceit, delight denied,
I've cried myself to sleep and not to wake,
     the rake of fake exposure
               drawn against my skin,
                    the sin
of emptiness is only not to love, and not
     to live a liar's dice in endless games
     of fixed abuse,
               the use, my love,
     is in the fluid of the stars.

HOMECOMING

You know how it is when we go
   to that place where we fuck like horses
   or the wild moaning of cats low in the grass,
   dragonflies locked in midair, the copulation of whales, mindless,
our eyes blazing, tongues firing flame,
   the fluids of our bodies passing back and forth
   in the dark, purling cup of our loins.
Certainly we are driven with passion,
   the lust of fusion gathering to a peak
   as we plunge backwards into birth,
   into the dark, murmuring heart of the mother,
   the great star-head of the father bursting
in a swarm of flowers, a flood of reconciliation.

Surely we know how it is,
   and yet how thoroughly desparate we become,
   over and over again, to break our bodies,
   to open our blood and drive our bones
into the hard security of reassurance,
   to make things right, to draw the line,
   to take possession of one another.
Thus we become careless and bored,
   we cling and yet we push away,
   we beat against the walls of our house,
   infuriated with ourselves, our children,
   our lives, the impeachment of our inclinations,
we bury our hearts below ground and fuck with our minds.

So how much better to find our bodies first
   within the landscape of our dreams,
   the earth held in the center of our chest,
   breathing inwardly and outwardly,
turning from darkness into light, returned
   to that undying portion of ourselves
   that never seeks completion, having none.
How much better to exchange the gift
   we have to give, the fluctuating radiance
   of our skin allowed to shine,
   our blood infused with dreams,
   our minds alive with light,
and then we fuck like horses, moan like cats,

we pass our human being back and forth,
   we arch within our lives without cessation,
   we bring our bodies home
to live at peace among ourselves.

ON THE LUNAR INFLUENCE OF THE WHITE GODDESS

As she vaults, beckoning, into the evening sky,
her belly curved, bright, beginning to grow;
as her arch bends like a bow against the stars,
Venus hovering nearby like a child, her bright point
illustrating the western descent, the dark air.

As she is grown by the sun we grow, we rise
upward through layers of sleep, the fire in her belly
shedding light, she grows larger with child;
we fill our lungs with dark air and dreams,
pivoting skyward from the recognizable earth.

We are drawn into the fullness of her bright circle;
we are dreamed in the center of the belly of the moon,
each time turning back into the stars, to darkness,
where once again the crescent, barely visible, begins to bloom.

Paul Wear

LOVE POEM

it's this window frame / crept up at the edge
where my substance spread feeling your thighs /
close to where there are no names at all /
name gone sighs / this window that moves
and someone said impossible / and i've stopped
waving my fists / and i am a caravan by your waves /
you have brought me here / i sail your delicate reaches /
hoarding your tiniest warmths / like sparks like soft
diamonds the wants and flows from my body / your sweat
drops glistening over you in my cheeks / changing my
voice about how i am a man and i am penniless and probably
illegal / words dancing around the cunt in my breast
where you are curled

THE BAJA ROAD
            for Lawrence

Tijuana brays pinball bullfight
madness in crass neon,
infectious ache in my side,
and we fall off
into dust and the long haul.
You haven't spoken for hours.
I'm pushed away from warmth
into heat. The road drags
on past the rich men's toy towns
and down grey rock,
pulling and driving our eyes
deeper into our skulls.

At night we argue.
Shrieking under trees covered with dust.
The blond girl you were
with the magic bowl turns away
as we make a kind of peace,
knowing each other's pain.
And then mountains,
beginning of tall cactus,
fists out of sand,
viejo, shimmering air
even on the peaks.
Down to Guererro Negro,
where Indians wandered,
believing in the coming of mighty beings.

They came and they came,
where the black steel bird
squats on the 28th parallel,
staring eyeless.
A hundred feet of Aztec nightmare
sucked from the underworld.
Grotesque angles make a sign
of the proud new road.
This thing is no dream
of heavenly being.
Will never see
as Old Gods
through eyes of their people.
Never see the Senora
whose heart wails
for five daughters
who died at birth
while her throat is silent
for work to be done.

Never see cara cara,
feet piercing red cactus,
wind lifting an occasional feather.
He surveys white sand
that grinds in her teeth,
and shares her secret
of living on dry teat of dune
where life cracks open
and spits in his mouth.

Darkness over all.
Sun penetrates,
but there is darkness
on the miles to Mulege
gorges flood with anger
twice a year and tear boulders
from the earth.
Then Loreto opens a seed.
White and green memory blends
with thirst in a jungle pocket.
We walk in the plaza
and I ache for a sign
though you smile beside me.
Here too, adobe remembers the blood.
Houses sag under its weight.
Tuburon shocks water
with his red poinsettias
under the placid arrangement
of Pemex signs and rubber trees
and sweet white missions.

We roll out of barrancos to La Paz.
And I, full of secrets, am still.
You are there, but I cannot see you.
I am still, like cara cara,
waiting while the boy in the station asks,
"Chicklets, Americano?"

BAJA — to the Chartered Bank of London,
            it means a fine new road and they
            bought Perez' land for twenty
            thousand dollars.
            New Year's Eve we
            shot off guns.
BAJA — to the militia, the word has
            always meant a casualty.

Lawrence Ferlinghetti

THE 'MOVING WATERS' OF GUSTAV KLIMT

Who are they then
                these women in this painting
                 seen so deeply long ago
Models he slept with
        or lovers or others
                     he came upon
     catching them as they were
                   back then
        dreamt sleepers
              on moving waters
       eyes wide open
     purple hair streaming
               over alabaster bodies
      in lavender currents
Dark skein of hair blown back
               from a darkened face
      an arm flung out
             a mouth half-open
        a hand
           cupping its own breast
   rapt dreamers
      or stoned realists
             drifting motionless
    lost sisters or
      women-in-love
     with themselves or others —
pale bodies wrapt
      in the night of women
   lapt in light
     in groundswells of
          dreamt desire
        dreamt delight
Still strangers to us
     yet not
       strangers
  in that first night
     in which we lose ourselves

  And know each other

SHORT STORY ON A PAINTING OF GUSTAV KLIMT

They are kneeling upright on a flowered bed
   He
       has just caught her there
             and holds her still
     Her gown
         has slipped down
             off her shoulder
He has an urgent hunger
        His dark head
           bends to hers
             hungrily
And the woman the woman
    turns her tangerine lips from his
      one hand like the head of a dead swan
       draped down over
            his heavy neck
       the fingers
         strangely crimped
           tightly together
   her other arm doubled up
      against her tight breast
    her hand a languid claw
         clutching his hand
    which would turn her mouth
            to his
   her long dress made
      of multicolored blossoms
        quilted on gold
   her Titian hair
      with blue stars in it

And his gold
       harlequin robe
          checkered with
            dark squares
  Gold garlands
       stream down over
         her bare calves &
          tensed feet
Nearby there must be
    a jeweled tree
      with glass leaves aglitter
       in the gold air
It must be
    morning
       in a faraway place somewhere
They
  are silent together
        as in a flowered field
   upon the summer couch
       which must be hers
And he holds her still
      so passionately
  holds her head to his
       so gently so insistently
  to make her turn
      her lips to his
Her eyes are closed
     like folded petals
She
 will not open
    He
     is not the One

Mike Finley

THE HIGH DESERT

All the other shadows have names, so why not this shadow.
In so far as.
In as much as.
The whole day was like that, the face in the mirror when
    no one was looking.
And then it slips off and falls to the ground.
It was a moment like all the other moments except it didn't
    end.
It just kept beginning and going and lasting, I thought it
    would stop but it wouldn't.
Never the less.
More over.
Yucca braids are skeleton snakes are ladders of filaments
    going up to space.
And I climbed on and hung on for dear life.
And knuckles were ratchets were spools in the spine that led
    gently to earth.
The truth of the matter.
As a matter of fact.
Strapped to the tree I was running and running, and all the
    crumbs fell from the taproot behind me.
Some race.
Planting names in the desert and praying for people and watering
    dust with a bagful of sand.
I ran until I dropped and then I dropped.
All the syllables were brothers and sisters.
All of the sounds were a family sitting at holiday dinner.
All of the mountains were cats taking naps lasting millions of years
    and all of the creatures were piles of stones at the edge of the
    end that could never begin.
News from the isthmus.
News from the heart.
It was that kind of day when the blood turned to tears that were
    flushed from the heart.
Passing by, friends had to pry my hands apart.

HOME TREES

This little town is called Amherst; *ham,* little town, *hurst,* in the woods.
I lived here until I finished high school.
There are quarries nearby.
When I was younger, and the quarries were fresher, trees grew from their
  floor.
Amherst: Sandstone Center of the World.
Now, twenty years later, the quarries are deep with spring and rain water.
What's left of the treetrunks are all rotten now.
And the water trickles upward still.
In twenty years the stumps will be under.
But when I was a boy I used to walk along the cliffs on Lake Erie, and
  the bushes beside me came up to my shoulders.
Twenty years later I'm smaller than ever, the bushes are trees and I'm
  thrown in their shadows.
When my mother married Richard she took us to nearby Vermilion, named for
  the red clay the Indians used to make paint with.
After the Indians had been subdued, my stepfather Richard's Polish father
  Frank bought land in the area, and planted poplar trees alongside the riverbank
  which was the site of the home we'd move into years later.
The poplar, a staple in Lombardy, Italy, is favored for its rapid growth;
  it is straight and tall, makes a great windbreak, and in the summer its
  leaves turn upward in the breeze and shimmer like dimes.
Twenty years later the quick-growing poplars are dead and chopped down
  and taking their place by the side of the house is the sweep of the willow
  trees' languorous arms.
Richard believes that the languorous arms are too heavy, however.
If there were a thunderstorm like the one that tore through in 1956, the
  willow might break and might puncture the roof.
So he's making plans to chainsaw it down in the summer or fall.
Visiting this summer, Rachel and I make a trip back to Amherst and Vermilion.
Here was the house I grew up in, I told her.
I told her how when I was little I played in the dozen or so acres of apple
  trees, peach trees, and cherry trees.
From the attic window I could see the Platos' house across the hill.
Twenty years later, the orchards are gone, their places are taken by houses
  that are lived in by middle executives of the Ford Motor Company in nearby
  Lorain.
Lorain, the Best Location in the Nation, Industry Invited.
And Rachel and I walk for hundreds of yards til we find a good place on the
  cliffs of Lake Erie to make love in and nap in the shade of two elms.

GOING BEYONDING

Music all afternoon.
Thinking's no help now.
The worst thing in heaven is boredom.
Maybe a census of the stuff in the house, the holes on the walls
     or the dead bugs behind the stove, maybe taking out the trash
     will make a difference.
Something is missing, that's the feeling I got when I woke up
     this morning and looked at my room.

This place is like every other place I've ever lived in.
I don't know why.

Why can't I go beyonding today?
Who am I asking, my mother?
Is she going to say No, you can't go, I have work for you to do?
I think sometimes about all the people in the world I don't know
     very well.
When you look at their faces it's like reading a sign.
No. Don't. Impossible.

All I can do is sweat it out.
I've done it before a hundred times.
Maybe tomorrow I'll sit on my porch and the waves will come lap at
     my shoes.
I want to hear the sound of the front gate closing, the sound of a
     shotgun cocking.
It will echo all day in my head.
And I'll walk down the sidewalk like a strange kind of animal, as if
     I were doused in some strange kind of fluid, beyonded at last, and
     glowing from an acquaintanceship with light.

POOR BAUDELAIRE

Poor Charles woke up to learn that the streets were knee-deep
    in something red.
He thought it was wine and went back to sleep.
An hour later he opens his eyes and feels his kidneys cool in
    his hands.
He's curious now and turns off his alarm.
Now he's feeling the table for his change and his keys and runs
    into his brain, soaking on a plate.
Now he discovers his pajamas, bound and gagged on the floor
    of his closet.
Now he pours a glass of blood and lights up.

This habit is vile, he says, brushing his teeth.
His fork is a crocodile killing his eggs.
He shot the thing and sunk it in his milk.

Early in the morning the sun goes down and the sky turns red.
The executed spiders dangle all day.
Charles Baudelaire inscribes on his napkin the site of the grave
    that he chose in his sleep.

Just before lunch he retires to bed.
The lamp in the dark rearranges the walls.
The beast in the peonies shuffles and deals.
The radium mask on the clocks eats the face.
Something red seeps through the cracks in the floor.

Charles and Lillian paddle their boat by the island of sunshine.
And underneath, the drowning boy locates a puddle of air.
I want my revenge, he thinks, and he strokes.
The bad jokes no one can ever forget.

IN THE NEW COUNTRY

The laws are very different here, and take some getting used to.

When you come to this place, no one will help you or show you around.

And it isn't because we are inhospitable.

It's just that none of us are in any position to tell anyone anything
for sure.

So when you arrive it won't be because you planned your trip well, that
you picked this place from a long list of names from a dozen brochures,
one of which had to be interesting.

I think you will understand when it happens.

It was about time, you'll tell yourself, so here I am.

All I can offer as advice is that you try and not be afraid.

Because this place is strange but not dangerous.

Please try and be friendly, try hard to be brave.

Although no one will be there to greet you, although you will wish there
were signs or directions, step forward.

This place is your new home.

When it welcomes you, open your arms.

A.D. Winans

FOR GENE FOWLER

remembering that last day in
austin texas walking
the campus grounds feeling
all my forty years feeling
how strange it feels to be
here and now to survive all
these summers

the muscles the bones
the cells changing dying
and somehow surviving
traveling through this strange
time tunnel where words
form slowly balance delicately
like a raindrop on a leaf
then speeding up like a train
toward an origin you cannot
remember because there is
no you to remember it

THE PARTY GOES ON

Humphrey Bogart is in my dreams
He is framed in stained glass
And Sidney Greenstreet has invaded
My living room devouring my food
Joining Jimmy Dean dressed in
Patent leather boots stolen
From Elvis Presley who "revs"
Up his motorcycle while
The keystone cops pound on
My door with napkins for warrants
Stuffing them into my SCM typewriter
Which has been sitting empty for years

Abbott and Costello are killing Texas
Cockroaches with Japanese silkscreen fans
While the vice squad plays monopoly
Refuses to pass go steals
$200 and takes refuge in jail

Shirley Temple is ten years old
Sailing the Titanic
General Patton trading her his toy soldiers
For a quick look up her dress

Groucho Marx pale but growing younger
Smokes cigars with Jack Benny while
Swapping tales of Ponce de Leon
and the fountain of youth

Tonto drops in from the porno flicks
Wrapped in an army blanket stolen
From a confused Linus
Surrounded by Custer's cavalry
And the Lone Ranger who is courting
Truman Capote's favors

Nixon-Dean-Haldeman and Ford watching
The all night puppet show
Each a pawn in the chess master's game

Watching the hanging body of Mussolini
Swinging from the chandelier

Cut down the body says
A priest drinking wine from
A goat's flask

Why? says Peter Lorre in
A monotonous voice

Everyone shrugs his shoulders
And the party goes on.

Ed Buryn

San Francisco 1976

Georgia Rainstorm 1976

Utah Roadside 1975

Wet Truck 1976

Out West 1975

New York 1976

New York 1976

New York 1973

New York 1974

San Francisco 1976

New York 1973

Above Miami 1976

Miami Beach Hotels 1976

Miami Beach 1976

Oregon Mother and Daughter, July 4, 1976

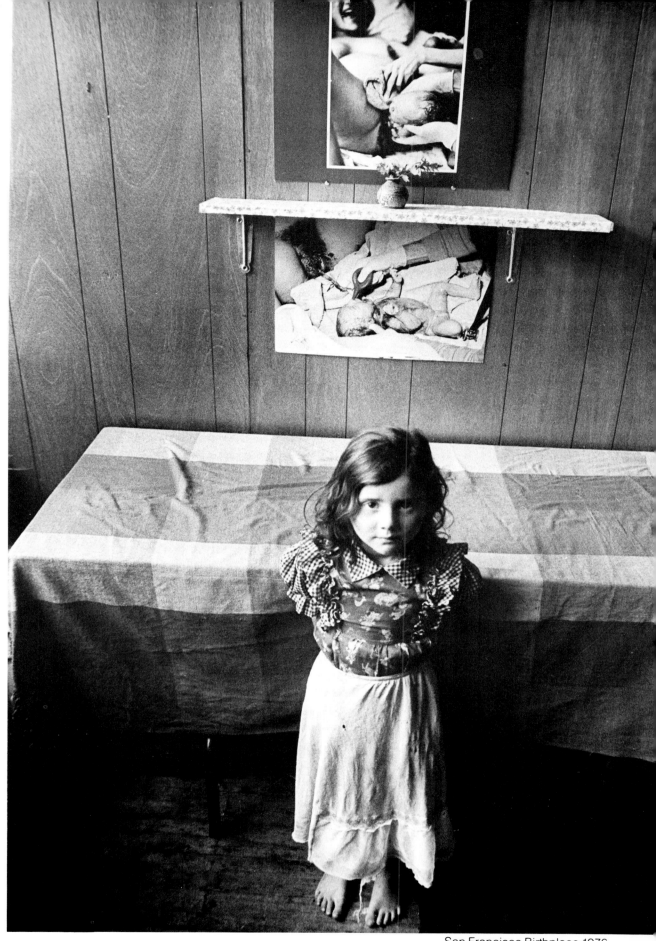

San Francisco Birthplace 1976

Safeway Liquor Department 1976

Santa Cruz 1976

Philadelphia 1976

Exhibitionism 1976

Eugene Lesser

THE DEMOCRATIC NATIONAL CONVENTION — 1968

1.   *"Hubert Humphrey is the articulate exponent of the human heart."*
    Joseph Alioto

Except through an appliance store window once or twice,
I had never even seen color TV before.
Everyone looked like they were wearing green suits.
Walter Cronkite was pretty cool, actually,
even though he didn't get the nomination.
Alioto said Humphrey was the articulate exponent of the human heart.

2.   *"Ken said if they nominated someone named Bogart*
    for vice-president, the ticket would be Humphrey-Bogart."

This casual reference in Eugene Lesser's journal,
made public finally after eight centuries of neglect
in the library of the Uranus Hilton,
sheds new light on the period before the Great Quake of 2155.
It is now widely believed that "Ken" is Ken "Kenny" Jacobs,
the mystery writer and creator of the beloved Inspector de Cartablanca.
The entry is undated but literary research strongly indicates
that it was written between the first great asterisk poems
and Lesser's brief love affair with the near-palindrome.
Dr. Patrick Gleeson, last February's astronaut-of-the-month,
points to the "fetishistic imagery, the rococo verbal texture,
the preciosity that appeased the salon critics of a gilded epoch."

3.   *"Chicago, thish great shitty."*
    The woman who read the roster

I don't feel like putting down the Convention.
I figure I'm it and it's me.
Writing a poem about the Democratic National Convention
is like writing a poem about the airport,
(which is, in turn, like an advertising agency
that has just landed the Chicquita Banana account).
Obscure.

BIG ME, MANKIND, AND THE UNIVERSE

One time, we were on mescaline,
Janet told me about the birds and the bees.
We were sprawled out on the back steps.
She told me as though I were eight years old
and for the first time I understood it all.
As a kid I thought a baby came out of the belly button,
and I remember getting a little pissed
when Billy Allen told me I came out of my "mother's cunt,"
(and that she had "innercourse" with my *father*).
I said, Hey Jim, watch what you're saying about my mother and father.
They talk about modern man knowing all the scientific answers
and that's why God is dead, because
nothing blows modern man's mind anymore,
(except sex and drugs).
But I'd like to go on record to say that I'm also modern man
and I don't know jack shit about anything.
Awe is my bag. Everything blows my mind.
Tonight I read in the sports section
about this local high school basketball coach
whose team is 0—13 so far this season. He said this:
"This has given me a tremendous amount of humility.
I was always humble, but now I am overly humble."
For me, I'd say I was always overly humble,
but now I am just humble.

AM I REALLY CUT OUT FOR THIS LINE OF WORK?

Most of my great lines never get written down.
Of course, many times they do.
For example, God is pitching a no-hitter,
and what about (fill in 2 or 3 other great lines).
I'm in the backyard, sitting in the sun.
All the plants and me pointing toward the sun,
except for when I turn slightly away to write this down.

JACK WEBB

Well, hi there.
Blah Blah Blah
(Imagine here the story of my life)
So what else is new?
My life story is very simple:
I came, I saw, I came.

THESE ARE MY POEMS

These are my poems.
This is my poem.
Once I picked up a hitchhiker
and when he got in I said,
"This is my car."

JUST A BOY AND HIS DOPE

I'm pulled over here by the back nine holes of the
San Geronimo Valley Golf Course and Country Club.
The cars are screaming past me.
I just bought a lid of grass for thirty five dollars.
A car whizzes by me and actually shakes my Dodge truck back and forth,
and now even a VW is shaking my Dodge truck,
and I'm thinking I must be stoned which I certainly am.
Thirty five bucks sounded steep at first,
but after a taste of the product I threw four tens on the table
and he gave me five singles back. Beautiful.
I've been working lately and today is payday.
I was looking for some primo shit and I found it, daddy.
Maybe I am enlightened.
I'm flipping, I guess. I never paid more than 15 or 20 for a lid.
Wait a minute (standup comic motif), that was a Lambretta
that just shook my Dodge truck (big laugh here).
I'm writing this on the back of mail received this morning.
Tim Tam Productions, LA pornography trip, sent me a brochure.
"Tim Tam has not forgotten you hardcore pocket book readers."
Ah, late Friday afternoon in the summer. After work. Really.
The question remains, as the cosmic and the mundane merge
on the horizon of my mind: Will the Giants ever get any pitching?

DRUG ABUSE IN MARIN COUNTY

*"Everything is a near-palindrome. Except palindromes.
There are only palindromes and near-palindromes."*
  Richard Nixon

Early this morning, Hawaii, runner-up at St. Moritz
and last year's most valuable near-palindrome,
was met by an ardent gathering at Kennedy Airport.
Hawaii, waving the silver medal obligingly for photographers,
hurled sharp criticism at the recently created CPC
(Concerned Palindromes Committee), a moderate group
of urban palindromes, co-chairmanned by Professor Otto Radar
and Doctor Bob Kayak, editor of ABADABA.
He dubbed them "palindromes unworthy of the name" and
included in his diatribe "riff-raff like nun and level."
Walking down the ramp he waved to enthusiastic admirers
and told one reporter, "wait till next year next till wait".
Hallelujah, considered by many to be the greatest
of all near-palindromes, and the only near-palindrome
ever invited to play in the East-West Palindrome Bowl,
was "shocked and abashed" by Hawaii's caustic remarks.
"Hawaii speaks for itself and not for the overwhelming
majority of decent near-palindromes. These are troubled
and tumultuous times. We must understand the many difficulties
that wealthier palindromes have in accepting us as a genre."
Countering hostile shouts of "Come off it, Hallelujah,"
the embattled six-time "Mr. Near-Palindrome" continued:

"I'm a loyal near-palindrome and always have been.
Only a blind anagram could believe otherwise."
The gathering stirred visibly at this reference and
for a moment it seemed as though violence were inevitable.
Two young oxymorons, carrying signs which read
"Anagrams Si, Near-Anagrams No", were attacked by
several beefy proper nouns, including Kleenex,
the so-called "mystery witness" in last year's PAP hearings.
Hallelujah spoke louder now as the throng began to turn away.
"I've been in touch with the near-anagram people
and believe me I am sympathetic with their grievances,
but we can't all expect to achieve genre status
without the slow and painful process of reason and caution.
These are tumultuous times and we must allow those
whom some of us would call enemies to undergo
the agonizing reappraisal of their convictions."
These were the last words audible. At that point,
the increasingly fervent crowd shouted Hallelujah down
with chants of "Madam I'm Adam" and in minutes
everyone, including airport personnel, photographers,
and bystanders waiting for their planes, began singing
"Palindrome, O Palindrome, We Feel Thy Rod Anew."
No serious injuries were sustained except for Ken Jacobs,
reported to be in only "satisfactory" condition
after being informed by a busboy in the airport coffee shop
that Ramon de Cartablanca was named Pagaent Magazine's
Junior College Athlete-of-the-Month.

I WOULD LIKE TO DO SOMETHING BEAUTIFUL, OUTSIDE OF EXISTING

Getting out of bed to write something down,
I add my name to the ancient list of people
who have gotten out of bed to write something down.
Jim Hagan, Tony Sidoti, etc.
Right now hundreds of people are getting up from
a warm electric blanket, just like I am,
scribbling down stuff like
God is on a Frederic March trip.

I'LL HAVE A CUP OF COFFEE AND A SLICE OF LIFE

Tony and this chick are driving real stoned and groovy
on a nice country road in Marin
where they pick up a long-hair hitchhiker
who right away hits Tony with the fact that
his front license is missing and that it's a big bust.
He's real uptight. Everything's a bummer or a bust.
So Tony thinks maybe he'll fire up and get the cat stoned
but halfway through the joint the cat says
that it's really a bust smoking in the car like that
and don't they know they could get busted.
Tony just trucks down the road and doesn't say much.
This guy, however, keeps saying one paranoid thing after the other.
A few minutes later, Tony looks at the rear-view mirror
and there it is, a CHP car with the red bubble blinking.
So Tony pulls over and when he rolls down the window
to talk to the cop who has walked over,
Marijuana smoke pours out of the car into the cop's nostrils
and Tony knew right there that the cop was making a split decision.
All that was happening in the cop's life,
and all that had already happened in the cop's life,
and other unconscious and hereditary and subliminal things
were all being sifted and weighed and judged
in this split second that was happening all around them.
So here it is: The cop is mellow.
He says you're missing your front license
and you should get one on soon. And split.
He didn't even want to look at Tony's driver's license.
Well, I thought, this is a story of the seventies. The first one.
The characters are the uptight hippy and the groovy cop.

EUGENE AND ONA

Me and my kid are hanging out at home tonight.
We're eating now.
She puts her foot in the soup. I frown.
My cuff, however, is in my own soup
as I reach across to write this down.
We're having a mellow dinner together.
My daughter loves to be ignored while she eats, and so do I.
I don't mind if you talk to me while I eat.
In fact, I enjoy it, as long as I don't have to look at you.
Or say anything. We're eating my split pea soup (with barley).
Ona picks up a cracker and looks at it with intense awe and delight.
She doesn't know it's just a cracker.
I tell her it's not cool to throw food on the floor.
She looks at me as though to say, "Oh, really?"
Ona is entering the supposed and so-called terrible twos.
I myself am deep into the terrible thirty sixes.
I try to emulate Ona.
To do my best, to do what I want,
to love openly, to live in the now,
and a few other biggies.
Someday I will be me.
And someday Ona will be Ona all over again.
This split pea soup is great.
Would you like a bowl?

I'M ALWAYS STONED WHEN I EAT SARDINES

I never actually think of buying sardines,
but every once in awhile I notice sardines
while I'm buying tuna fish
and I think, Oh groovy, and I buy sardines.
Then one day I'll be hungry
and there won't be much in the house
and I start opening this cabinet and that cabinet
and, all right, I notice a can of sardines.

* * * * * * * *

I'm trying not to think.
I'm thinking about not thinking.
I'm eating matzo (heavy on the butter and salt)
and sardines.

* * * * * * * *

Everytime I look at my checkbook I think I've sold out.
Not because I'm rich, you understand,
but just having a checkbook, having a checking account.
You know what I mean?
I'm eating sardines and I'm very stoned.

EUGENE ("GENE") LESSER

When I was a baby my father brought me into a bar
and said to the bartender, "Put a head on it."
Seriously, though, today is the first day of autumn.
At one point today I thought,
Here I am shampooing our rug with a shampooing machine
I rented from the Lucky Market in Fairfax.
Is this the same person who dot dot dot,
thinking of all the far out things I did
when I used to be far out, when everyone I knew
was wearing their underwear inside out
to get two extra days out of them.
On the chair, Freddy and Jane curl up in a Cancer glyph.
Bruno sleeps on his side on the rug.
I'm going to get in bed with Janet, who's warm and toasty
under the electric blanket (which I'll lower)
and watch the David Susskind Show.
I'm letting it all hang out here.
Fuck it, man, I've already paid my dues.

James L. White

THE ABSENCE OF WALTZING

I walk around these cold rooms
trying to remember if it is sorrow or light
that brings me to her small face
and ribs I want to play like forbidden chimes.
I walk the cold alone
and know it is sorrow
that brings me to the light.

My emptiness festers into a Sunday forever like old skin.
I want to believe in the little girl beyond my needs
in darkness.
Bring her into light like a tablet washed by sun
where she can finger up each contour of my disparity.

A gray mist comes from the gray park below as I write:
"A gray mist comes from the gray park below.
The little girl rides a naked horse gray,
rides blood red over his back
in the gray park, in the gray naked snow."

It is Sunday.
It is Sunday forever and begins to snow.
I am going into the snow as I have wanted to do for years.
I am going into the waltz like snow
where the little girl, the blood horse ridden gray
and my absence seem to dance forever.

VACATIONING

This is the total dark baby
where silence tears like an incision.
The motel bed is made for battle
where we fuck through mounting solitude.

I want to dream of a boy running
or running like a boy
to a still place in winter.

Near dawn I hide my truth to fit our waking hours
and ask if we should continue.
Your indifference is comforting in the rose light
as we drive to the ruins of another people.

SLEEPING ALONE

We sleep in this frail rib boat ramparting the vast,
so tightly, wearing nearly the same skin.
I question who owns my breath,
if you too dream of my father's funeral
where all the dahlias bled.

Somewhere between sleep, dream, and death,
I kiss the hair of your chest, mixed with seaweed and moss,
then fight to wake, thrusting upward,
taking the air alone as I must
and know we are strangers wearing nearly the same skin.

It's morning and the apartment's cold.
The moon still hangs by the factory like worn taffeta.

A PSALM FOR CONTINUING
for Dana Christian Jensen

[1] *Sharks Burning*

Nickel rooms are like old blues
filling the air with stale space and neon.
This bloated body and walls sweat and cough
some briar of memory into the peeling halls.

Dying here would be good enough
by a stranger smothering this heart's sad fire,
releasing these body waters into earth
where I would change from guilt to calcium and lime.

I hunt my streets near evening.
The sun more innocent than a little girl's thigh
touches this old regret called town,
Ruby's Shine Parlour, The Loneliness Cafe,
an old Negro porter dozing
before the final train.
Summer's too long here
like a maiden aunt staying an extra day.

Now the high voltage night.
Library Hotel winos search
the trash for their swollen souls.
I go to the French Illusion Movie House
where reels of tarnished meat hump the air.
It is shark air and we are sharks burning.
Old men doing things to themselves under their coats,
dreaming of some dear necrophilia with their long dead.

I seek the heat of transient hands
working my thighs into dust,
hanging like limes in blackness,
burning from the weight of Sundays,
burning with some longing for death
that would slam my lids of eyes forever.

I come with another shark into pitiable darkness,
wanting to be water into stream into river into nothing.

[2] *Supplication*

Christ.
Jesus Christ.
Christ of worn days.
Jesus of all lonely rooms on this earth.
Sweet Christ, just one little hit.

[3] *Weaving Rain*

By now things have no reason,
timing rivers or the way of shadows,
my stopped life with nameless sharks,
and five dollar rooms where things have no reason.

Then someone enters so simply,
wearing rain,
a coat of wind,
and bone shirt dark as wanting.
He had traveled long through silence
for sorrow was in his dance.

I spoke of this cracked life,
the failures,
people leaving in September,
of seeing one eagle and lying of the rest.

In my fortieth year he allowed me to breathe and even sleep,
changing my sullen humors and harrowed nights,
my hollow rooms of ribs, marrow, and solo skin,
into a psalm for continuing.

[4] *Psalms and Beatitudes*

Praise each thing you will know always:
the taste of salt,
the first wind of August,
the darkness of sleep,
the comedy of morning,
the humor of clocks,
those who wear rain.

Blessed are the children of wind,
those tied to strings of hunger,
all fast dancers and poets,
all night truck stops,
those who have traveled to Missoula by bus,
and you who give your flesh as healing.

This is our jubilate,
the temporal compounds of light,
the movements of fantastic dance.

Amen, amen.

Dana Christian Jensen

FINDING OUR WAY
for Jim White

Love,
wet lips against the ice iron dark,
tears his flesh away.
He drops one bead of blood, one of semen
on the Navajo blanket,
shimmering stars
in the universe woven of brilliant wool.
The following spring he gives birth
to a full grown bear.

Sky turns from the withered hand,
sun gets up in his teats
to nurse the creature
like sucking flame burnt green.
He and the animal become the hunters of summer
filling themselves wild with berries,
smearing honey and mud into their loose groins.
They mate standing.
Heaviness pulls his shoulders groundward.
Shush-bah-toah,* there is more speed on four legs
and the loss of balance changes the shape of his head,
drives him up stream against the anger of claws,
the new language of his long tongue.

*Navajo for bear by the water

What hangs in the night
with aging stars
now tells them through the running grass:
survive so many ways
down to the white instinct of root.

By now his flesh sags
as Autumn falls in its fatal beauty.
Quiet as leaves turning
they circle on the ruined path,
their weak dance toward the final season.

With the first great snow they go howling,
away,
fires consuming themselves to certain extinction.
They wander the woods all night
and only in the silver dawn
he lies down in the silent whiteness.
Everywhere a last breath falls.

A dark thing stands long
over the still form in snow,
then kneels,
ripping him throat to crotch, open and steaming,
stares hard into the ruptured sky
mouthing the long vowels of sorrow,
and takes a deep draught of flame from fire waning
in the dead one's gut.

I WAKE IN THIS CABIN

My love impenetrable,
sleeping well within her own body,
delicate carpel in a dream-rose.
The furnace ignites with a sudden breath,
its small window flaming
like the postcard of a forest fire.
My motions, intrusions into a cold world,
stepping down the dark tunnels of my pants,
and forcing the door
over its wedge of packed snow.

Out here
moon sets a path of light at my feet.
I walk
collapsing brittle snow into black patches,
moving fire, leaving small holes of ashes.

In a circle of dry grass
surviving above snow, I stop,
stare back at my footprints
unable to account the distance between them,
where I'm lost
or moving toward what I stalk
through sleep, books and silence.

In the cabin a light goes on.
She wonders where
I am
yellow in my poverty
          terrible as these weeds.

POEM

Sensing death you took your body out
into miles of night.
Where falling leaves cover you
you take your last breaths.
You are gone like the moon off water.

This dawn broken,
this morning bright and hollow
a spider crosses warm rock
where my light fingers moved on your neck.
There are no face and hands to cover with my tears,
no breasts to wash and kiss away,
no body to mourn in my arms,
only the flow of water leaving my bones,
my skin shrinking to cover me alone.

THE PLAIN MOON

It ends here.
The final wish breaks my open hands.

I've learned a long way down
into fires untended on a frozen lake.
Take me, I ask, from the dark rings of iron
where I seek your waist and tongue
enough to open me
like this poem burned from the center.

But you are too young to play us again
beyond this reasonless night.

Tracking elegant holes
only the snow will fill,
you lose your ring to say
night takes from us all.

So I tell you, Erin, my love
is plain as the moon
pulling water over you.
You give breath to it;
your dark words roll in from far away
crashing down on the small life within me.

The ring is never found
and I leave you in streetlights,
frozen glares on puddles
and return to what is left:
the long feel of cold in the small of my back,
a ladder through my poems that no one climbs.

My ribs, a fault beneath the earth,
shift; buried
I see you coming down on me
and turn your slender legs to wood
in the oblong grain of my mind.
Surviving back to hands
I bare my empty thighs
up into a rail of breath
and hold myself like bread saved
for another winter bird.

Douglas Blazek

NIGHTLOG

Somewhere over China the pink
membranes of dawn are thinning and
people everywhere are beginning to snap about
wringing sunlight over their bodies

but here in California
darkness clogs the air
a charcoal arm blindfolds the horizon

grass pulls silver thread from its ears
flowers bend low and listen to god-sounds
trees toughen their roots by drinking bone minerals
trains in the Western Pacific yard mate like bulls
tons of deep sound tumble toward bedrooms

stones in the soil clench their souls
houses are noisy quarrels of sleeplessness
clocks froth at the mouth
the past is put into a plaster cast
age clamps its hot breath around a chest

little that is done is cool water

in his pajamas homo sapien is kissed by
a sudden slab of meat
he learns it to be his own carcass

NIGHT VISION

Night rustling
frustrated
a dog with no tongue
trying to bark

sleepers desperately putting
their heart to their ears
talking stars gathering
beyond moons
crowding into a brilliance
known only to blood

a swarm of
thoughts
evaporates its light
heading west
never stopping

and in the morning
that air
so astonishingly
intelligent!

MIGRATIONS OF CONSCIOUSNESS

All day long my ears sleep
clenched like camellia buds
they do not hear any talking
only the movement before things speak:

the world is not yet put together

time is non-functional
and solid
like a metal thought lying
in a desert

stars are all by themselves in a box
lakes float aimlessly in the air
flowers swim in the roots of mountains
animals of every variety are stuck in trees

slowly they realize their
misplacement
and are stealthily moving
like the pass of a magician's
hand over his hat
to their rightful
place

upon their return
I wake up
and set the alarm
in you

LITANY OF THE BODY

I am here for the moment
in my forehead

all my thoughts rolled into a
period of light
this exit at the end of the world

*

Now I am in my fingers

beauty is placed upon
stretchers of my palms and
the pallbearers of my fingers
carry it to my mouth

if its edible its beautiful
a definition
also the reclaiming of what the body
thinks is rightfully
its

*

Now I am in my chest
where the stranger pours his voice to
the farthest extremity

how he loves to hear himself
from these points returning to the hub
all rivers meeting on a button

*

Now I am in my feet
or perhaps my feet are in my mind

both are travellers
one walks through my body
down my legs
out the world
to bring it back from that
reverse direction

the other is a master at getting lost:
the usual rescue party arrives
and builds a city on the spot

*

Now I am in the paper you hold
in your hands

these words as I continue to
make them appear before your eyes
arriving sure as bodies
snapping to attention from seed

they live for the nano-second it takes
to watch an idea perform

then turn to pillars

*

Now I am vanishing

entering the air
the vanish of all things vanished
this synapse between pillars

and the next thing you do

RAPPORT

All that is in this room
moves their x-rays
through me

my cells are bombarded with
telepathy

a print is made
doctors would call it bones

I call it applause

THE STORM

Time has been scraped raw
wind finds an unpleasant wetness in its throat
a dark drill is boring to the center of light
it will rain

wings will be strewn across the fields
my voice will slip onto my foot like a shotput
under the earth huge capes rustle

an intumescence broods within casual things
they are capable of taking lives

it will happen

Judith Anne Greenberg

IN THIS HOUR

In this hour
a woman is being born
She will have many dreams
She will be lonely
She will dance before her mirror
with her feet of clay

It will be many years
until she knows

THE ROAD

It is an evening in autumn
and a white horse is walking
down a country road
He is alone
He is silent
He is leaving his pain behind him

THE PEACOCK

a peacock cries in the forest
and a green eyed insect
lands on my hand

this is a dream I shall have

this dream of sorrow
and bright wings

LOOKING FOR YOU

your cousin alison
arrives on the coast
in a yellow convertible

she is looking for you

you are sitting by the barn
you have grown thin as a boy
you have forgotten how to speak

ANOTHER LAND

In november the wars began
Many were dying in the village
and our fields were burning

Yellow butterflies were flying south
We watched in silence
Their wings darkening falling

HANDS

You leave me sleeping on the beach at Ventura
This is the last time I ever see you
A cold white fog
and a dead pelican floating out to sea

I am dreaming my name is Anna
and you are rich and careless
I can tell by your hands
that you love me

HEART

The heart of a man
is an open door
where antelope are running

They are graceful as wind and flowers
They are hungry

LOVE

Without hands or heart
this hour of no beginning

Once deer gathered
in the darkness of my lawn
and the tender breath of birds

These mountains are kneeling
They are made of stone
They are made of wings

Door of the soul you are soundless

THE ORCHARD

I remember the last time
a ship sailed into harbour
everyone was on it

a movie star from guatemala
and all my childhood friends

someone said the war had ended
and a one legged soldier
danced on the table

in the moonlight
the quivering horses
were drunk on fermented apples

I slept that night
beneath the trees
with my fair skinned lover

I think it was autumn
and we were happy

Frank Graziano

DESEMBOQUE
for Buzz and Kris

We have learned there is nothing
but fish, some sandy eyed,
and the others
only bones, off-white and vacant,
like underwear.

When we made it over
the last nippleless
hump we dropped our packs
and the sea offered its fat lap
so we took it.
We talked about things
we would do before we died,
and that was good,
but the narcoleptic sun
gave up, and the mesquite was dry,
so we burned it.

Then, as if out of nowhere,
I fell asleep
and was glad, and the stars
were their same miserable selves
tearing off the sky.

LOS CORCHOS
for Laura

The horizon gave up,
and like sperm, like a submerged ball
the moon plunged toward the sky,
and the darkness seemed shell-shocked,
leaped into crab holes.

There you are: your breasts
leaning to their respective sides,
your chest flat and two toned,
like a masked tortilla. Around us
the fire has pitched its tent,
so we sit in it.
Everything we can't say echoes.
Even if we were fat
there would be something missing,
something hollow, like a corpse
with no death in it.

No matter. There you are,
and the smell of mackerel blows in
from Sestea. As the fire
burns down,
and the tent shrinks around us,
there is nothing but the sound
of your brush, your sound
closing in like a mangrove.

AHAB AND THE WHITE BERET

You have learned the lesson
of the fishery,
that the earth is surrounded
by a white film, and that the stars,
like ulcers, are proof of this.
Someday the blanket
will unwrap the earth
and that day will be everyone's
birthday. A disk
will form and hover over everything —
like the skin that forms
over boiling milk.
Call the disk Heaven.
Take the disk and put it
in your lip, or roll it like a chart
and make a leg out of it.
Build an altar
of maidenhair fern, then buy beams
and mold a ship around it.
Repeat to yourself:
blubber, like God, is everywhere.
Remember Munch,
who put his arm in a grandfather clock,
but didn't swing it.

HIGHWAY OF THE DEAD

If you want to die don't come here.
In Teotihuacan nothing changes,
the sun is a mango, peeled
but not eaten,
something perishable that won't rot.

When you come here no one will notice.
Rain will welcome you
with its ridiculous password.
A heaven of bodies
will be stagnant around you,
a fraternity of the miserable,
and now you are one of them.
Like a leaf in vaseline,
like a scorpion in a paperweight,
you'll live forever in mouthfuls of granite,
propped up in your grey suit,
your stale soul crumbled
like the center of pastry,
flaked from your body.

When your children come they won't know you.
Your wife will be happily dead somewhere.
But now you are an ancient,
your eyes held open and full of hallways,
your face pushing forever
the same mossy whiskers out of stone.

THE LEGEND OF WUPATKI RUIN

When the sun has
finally pulled out its hair
the Sinagua send out
one ear, a scout, a dried
apple looking in the night
for sound. If everything
is still the earth is
unbuttoned and first come
the children, then women,
then the men with their hoes,
their cheeks red
as adobe. After the black
seeds are planted everyone
waits for the moon
and when harvest is finished
they return to their molten
coats, to their hair
locked in lava.
When the sun rises
lizards hide the evidence
in bristle cones. Fingers
sprout cautiously in the shade,
breathing like mushrooms.

Gino Clays Sky

DUENDE DE LAS SIERRAS

FOR MARIA ALANIZ

he moon was full in the solstice rising fat into the summer. Maria and I were high in the Sierra following the streams and rivers, moving slowly through the forest—camping whenever the place looked right—as a slow migration into ourselves.

One night, after we had finished supper, we were passing a bottle of tequila back and forth with short speeches between each pull on the bottle. Gutteral sounds. Deep and animal just before the warmth would hit the stomach to smooth the express to the brain. It felt good to have the tequila fire in the body—allowing the body to dance, and the tongue to wander with a crazy happiness. "Oh boy," I said, "it feels so good to be here." I must have said that for every camp, but this one was different—it had a strange, haunted magic to it—like a secret hiding place for robbers, or forest spirits.

For two weeks we had been following the eyes of each day. Two people with everything. We were free to wander without direction—holding a sweet euphoria inside a new love moving as the imagination flirts itself into strange canyons and rivers—over mountains, and the long slow motion slide down the hill to the rainbow's laugh. It was all perfect, and good. The beauty of two souls unhaunted by old radios; or the magnetic pull of the genes to produce a like example. Later that night when the fire was still strong I looked into your face and I saw another generation—your last incarnation, or the one before. And I saw myself there with you living in the mountains deep inside a marriage—working the earth with the seasons. I kneeled down before you, and removed your boots. . . rubbing your feet telling you a story with my hands.

Did I wash your feet that night one hundred years ago?

I saw us never leaving the mountains—staying in the Sierra. Horses, a cabin with a smoker in the back. Clothes made from deer and elk skins, and blankets woven from our own hand-made loom. Mountain grouse, trout, and vegetables from the garden—holding out through the white winters chasing footprints watching for the first signs of spring: Ground-hog's day, the Equinox carefully celebrated; and then the first spring thaw. . . the breakup, and the long johns went back into the trunk. We started the garden on the fifteenth of June: the root vegetables went in on the full moon, and the toppers went in on the New. I watched the sweat run down your face and arms as you were weeding the garden with your straw hat pulled far into your shade. I became aroused pulling you down into the furrows licking the sweat from your body. The summer storms came booming with fire.

Did I wake up the memory that night? The ghost of the hidden fire? The tequila was gone, and we were deep into the night. The fire was only coals, and the stars were full of night Gods exploding stories and visions. I heard horses—a whinny, deep and heavy, and then the tongue-click of the riders moving the animals up the ridge above the camp. I could see a woman lighted by the moon. . . Indian, maybe Mexican. The man was older. . . a mountain man with long hair wearing a long buckskin coat. Were they looking for their camp. . . their cache? You were awake, moving closer to my body, and my muscles tightened around my ancestors. My grandmother had told me stories about the ghost-spirits of the soul dwelling inside body dreams. I was frightened, excited, wanting the ultimate: a showdown—the duel reaching for the coup. Were they trying to come into our bodies? And then they were gone. . . the horses' hooves soft in the alpine grass moving away.

In the morning we were unusually quiet—breaking camp after coffee—touching each other with fingertips, and soft, deep eyes holding on to the feeling—wanting to stay, but we kept on packing our gear. There are places in the oceans where ships disappear, and there are places in the mountains where bodies leave into the spirit of their ancestors and never return. It must be too good to ever want to come back. How close were we. . . how close? That was our last night in the mountains. We headed for the Pacific. . . leaving the vision without translation.

What life were you? What life were you before? What life were you before my bride? My woman, my wife singing Mexican songs as you cooked on the open fire, planting the earth with your music and feet.

Did I wash your feet last night?

Did I kiss your eyes?

Did I make love to you, Maria?

Did I make love?

Was it two weeks we spent together, or a lifetime? How old do our bodies stay with the earth holding the spirit of the dream? When did we leave, and when did we begin? How long did we ride that night, Maria? How far did we chase the Duende?

IDAHO
AN INDIAN WORD TRANSLATED
INTO COWBOY
GUNS, STEAKS, AND PICK-UP TRUCKS

"ey Cowboy!"

The words came shooting out at me like a wild crack from a hungry bullwhip. I spun around in a low crouch suddenly caught up in the quick-draw game. Once again, the old theatrical six-gun came spinning out of my imaginary theater. Twenty yards in front of me was my old high-school sidekick. The hero of everyone's yearbook, and he was laughing just like a summer thunderstorm. He still wanted to know who was the fastest. He had been the football star, all-state bulldogger, and champion blue-ribboned shit-disturber, and the first of our class to be rewarded with a shotgun marriage. He didn't care. He loved all noteriety as long as it put his name in the newspaper. He stood in the middle of the street looking like a Grade A side of beef waiting to be judged. He drew on me, and it was all over.

"Blam, splat. . . you're dead, Cowboy!" He jumped on top of me riding my back down the sidewalk, hitting me over the head with his huge fists, and waving a cherry and maple gun rack to everyone who would stop to watch. He saw the whole world as either a mouth or an asshole, and I felt like one dumb asshole. He jumped off my back and started to herd me into The Silver Dollar Restaurant and Bar, with the illegal poker game riding low and smoky in the back room.

I had tried to sneak in the back door of my home town, but I missed. I had left on the run, and I didn't want to see anyone, especially my ghosts. I needed some time just to think about this leather-faced, shitkicker town stuck in the middle of an Indian reservation. And there I was, trapped by my old buddy, and future roadshow Governor. Old Motormouth.

"Damn and Goddam, it's good to see you! How long has it been? Ten years. Yeh, I remember. You ran off with that professor's wife to Santa Fe. I could never figure that one out, old Buddy. You were one of the top line drivers in the Teamster's. That's the trouble with this state. As soon as anyone learns how to read, they leave town. When was the last time you had a steak?"

Bourbon and water with a beer back came sliding down the silver dollar bar. I knew it was just the beginning. A condemned man for having two ears that work. He was booming right out of his chute, and digging in his spurs for an afternoon of riding ears.

"Hey Buckaroo, I've got me three gas stations now, and I'm starting an excavation company. . . moving old mother earth. How about that, Cowboy? And I'm making loads of money. . . ha, ha. I jus' bought me a brand new Case backhoe with a three yard bucket. I could move Old Baldy right down to a nubbin with three big bites and one good, clean spit. Cut it right, and pour in the concrete. Presto! Chango! . . . and we've got ourselves a fine lookin' trailer park. If I could get that mountain moved, we could have at least one more hour of sunlight. And that's one hour of work, which means a lot of the long green. I was going to do it. I even had the city council all ready to go, but those asshole ecologists moved in from the University and put a stop to it. Said it was some sacred Indian bullshit. What the fuck do they know? They've got so much hair they can't think straight. You wait and see, Cowboy, they're going to ruin this state yet. Hey! I jus' bought me a Chevy C-10 with three-hundred and eighty cubes in the plant. I took off that fucking air pollution device and threw it into the river. Look at that gunrack! . . . ain't it a honey?"

I couldn't figure out why in the hell I was standing at the bar listening to his bullshit. I hated all of his ideas, but I was fascinated with the way he could shift gears. The Ramrod.

"I jus' spent two thousand smackeroos for a custom Browning twelve gauge with a rosewood stock. I had old Jim carve a Peterbilt tractor on one side and a potato cellar on the other, with one of our good Idaho sunsets going down right over the cheekrest. Hell, you've got to put your money into something. It ain't worth a spinster's fart in a tornado in the bank. Guns and steaks. That's where to put it. I've got me four walk-in freezers full of venison and beef. All Idaho beef fed on good Idaho grass. God's grass, and wild alfalfa right off the summer range up around Salmon."

Another bourbon and beer were coming down the bar. The bartender looked like he had a mural of the Painted Desert air-brushed on his nose—the only color on his face. Shit, I thought, picking up the beer, somehow I've got to get out of this place. Ramrod was just beginning to get warmed up, and he was coming at me like a brahma bull through a wheat field bucking his jaws wide open.

"Oh Damn!" he said, as he finished a can of beer in one swallow, "I bet Marge would love to see you. Remember her? The little blond cheerleader with the big jugs. We've been married fifteen years this summer. Knocked her up on Senior Sneak Day. Goddam! That was right in the backseat of your old man's car. How about that! Remember the time we blew up the outhouse on Halloween? Stole the dynamite from your old man. How's the old bastard anyway? . . . still peddling guns? Dead? Well shit, Cowboy, you can't win 'em all. He was sure a good old bastard. I bet he could never figure out where you came from. Not from his balls, I bet. I always figured you were a bit strange myself. Especially the time you wouldn't fuck that sheep we had tied to that electric-barbed fence. But you could sure shoot. . . give you credit for that. Do you think they'll ever outlaw guns? Hell no! It'd be like outlawing pussy, or Jesus. I've got two years supply of food in the basement, and twenty cases of ammo. They'll never take me."

"Who's they? I said, hoping he wouldn't try to answer my question. I was counting the dollars cemented into the bar. I already knew, but I didn't know what else to do. He didn't even slow down. Old Motormouth, and by this time I couldn't even remember his name.

"I've got four trail bikes ready to head for the mountains, and two snowmobiles hidden away once I get there. Come on, let me buy you a three inch steak. Let's put some sting back into your ass. . . get you rollin' those big rigs again. Hey! Why don't you move back here and work for me. . . running my backhoe. You used to be really sweet with one of those honeys. The best. Jus' get yourself a haircut, and some decent clothes, and go to work. Quit foolin' around with that writing business, and those professor's wives."

"Yeh," I said, taking out a pane of pure-light acid and touching it to my tongue. "I could pick strawberries with a three-yard bucket without bruising a one. But doing that kind of work is like fucking sheep backed up against an electric-barbed fence. Know what I mean. . . Cowboy?"

Aram Saroyan

LOVE

The beauty of a summer evening . . .
The television on in the living room: "The Waltons."
A book I like out there too.
But I sneak away to catch the day fading
Into the first minutes of the night.

To be a survivor of all this richness
And to live on, cherishing life, for its own sake.
Singing praises to its light and its night,
The pungency of color in a child's face,
The birth of ideas in the mind.

Outside the fog closes the scene in —
Pale mists the trees move behind.
Closer, the daisy bush just outside this window
Is immobile — the crowd of flowers
Stopped in windless color.

Empty, empty, as I am now —
As I always feared before but now merely notice.
I am time, not space; time to engage
In conversation, gentle interaction, with space.
To make love with the sure touch of time's favor.

No rush, no necessity to be finished —
An understanding with the world of pleasure
That is time itself — the pressure of a hand
Just so, no more the man than the woman,
And no more one another than love.

POEM

I don't want to be a seer
And fly through the universe
I just want to be a man
And stay here
And let my time be open
To your time as yours is
Open to mine
And the children grow up
Inside our lives
And the house goes through
Its karma
And friends and neighbors
Successes and failures
Birds and learning
All intertwine within
The daylight and the nightime
And I look out to see
The same tree
Differently each time

SNOW IN CALIFORNIA

My daughter's enterprising little spirit
Bestows its gift upon the virgin air:

What excitement the whiteness makes in her!
She clasps it in her mittens

Until it's a snowball which she doesn't throw,
But lingers over, having never before held snow.

THIS IS WHERE WE LIVE

This is where we live
This is where we spend our days
The hours grow on us here
And take us where we are going

The light in the garden
The food in the kitchen
The water from the faucet, dripping
The stories have been told and will be told again

The face of the mother
The back of the father
The laughter of the little daughter
The sensation of being alive in time right now

THE NIGHT

The night is so
empty, and bright,
filled with thin air
and tiny stars deep
in the distance
that is infinite,
that has no end
like no mind, and yet
here I am, within it,
here, breathing, alive
and thoughtless
as the stars themselves.

POEM WRITTEN DOWN IN THE DARK

I lie in bed
listening to the dogs bark,
a cold holding my
right ear in
some kind of grip.

You asleep,
Strawberry in her
sleeping bag on
my right,
Cream in her little
bed on your left.

A family!
And I have just put the cats out
finding them cuddled too
close to Cream
not to wake her
one of these minutes.

They're out on the roof now,
looking in from time
to time
at their mysterious
owners.
I cough and blow
my nose;
you stir to the other
side of the bed . . .

A dog howls,
frogs croak —
there is a thickness
to the earth
— to life —
so much is here.

We strain
to keep our bills
paid, to make
our way up the ladder
of success, but
what is here is here
now, no less
than when we are millionaires.

I'm glad I'm a poet.
It's not a job,
but a calling — the
sort of thing that
made me go downstairs
naked for the
pad and the pen,
keeping the universe
in motion.

Now it's quiet
but for a lone
cricket.

No better than that —
no more or less
than a man awake
when he should be
asleep in a
rich night, listening
to his child breathing
beside him, not
ready for sleep.

LIFE IS NO ARRIVAL

Life is no arrival. The day goes,
Turning into night, reading — an arrival
Of a kind, I guess, if a book is good enough,
If it can fix life in its lines; as if life
might ever offer the time for its own vision,

Revealed. But the action *is* an understanding,
Day in and day out, courting power, courting doubt.
The child works tirelessly each day learning the human
Vocabulary. She sleeps as we do, wakes fresh
For another bout with her angel and adversary.

Writing is only another thought too deep for
Thinking, moving into the moving lines before
It is known, before it is understood. Poetry
Surrenders to its flow, unknowing, innocent.
These lines are written on the run.

LIFE IS A DREAM

Life is a dream.
Boulders on the beach assume the form
Of animals. No man is certain. Death
Speaks in the wings, coaching, prompting

Emotion, the love of wood
Burning, the child's face waiting, laughing.
The sun comes up so many times, lighting
The life that is there to be seen.

We have been traveling through this tunnel
In eternity. Rocks persistently speak
To us, saying something so pure it is only
Feeling. This and that, this and that.

The buildings of the mind shut down
Before the advance of this truth.
We are here for good. There is no one
To be us instead. We are alive and dead.

Helen Nestor

Michael Wolfe

THE MAN WHO COULDN'T SLEEP NIGHTS

Milkmaid in the cow's belly.
Wino inside a grape.
Children calling *come
out, come out where*

you are.

*

Everything
to one who waits,
except borders.

*

Sleep, as another country.

*

Ocean cables
placing calls to themselves
cross my pillow.

*

Trans-pacific static.
Garbled dreams.

*

"Hello?"

      "Hello."

*

Drowning in wide awakeness.
Flotsam,
and then some.

*

Bedroom walls, splintered light:
passing brights of fast cars
stripping woodwork back
then disappearing.

That Defoe
speaks of Rob. Crusoe
as 'rescued'.

Did men sleep soundly then,
when lids fit tightly?

*

Leaps one makes
adding figures,

better than counting sheep.

Zero to the tens column,
six and six are
twelve

and eight makes
twenty.

*

'Twenty centuries of stoney sleep'

*

Where Wharf Road
runs down to the sea

another man
in a large van

who meant to drive on
into the night

seeing no safe place in sight
cranks the wheel hard

left, heading out of town
back where he came from.

AT THE NATIONAL HOTEL
              for Joe Dillard

Make a world
where things work out
so each man meets his need

and no one pays for it.

That's all I ask.

                    *

In Satan's day of falling
how did he rate it?

EARTH IS ADAM'S KINGDOM.

THINGS HERE COST.

                    *

"One bloody castle,"
the fat diner said.

                    *

Famished eyes
roll backward
in the sockets.

                    *

Lightning: Cross & beacon.
Then it's gone.

                    *

Every night a dark story.
Flaps slam in the tents of desert Bushmen.
I move around a window
looking in.

A finite echo
locked in space
between heart-beats
says

    "The family is large.
    But there are groups.
    In my group
    all the men are dying."

                    *

Says

    "The Beautyful Ones
    are not yet born."

                    *

Says

    "A dream has
    dreamed us."

                    *

On ripe nights
reading Gideon's
the begat section of Genesis
strikes me as short.

A LONG BETWEEN

Bounty that works itself free of your hide.

*

Words in a world
being born
            where things just born
are never ready.

*

It follows a course
not of stars
            but selves
we separate
   (some stuff museums with)

*

The trouble with the Truth,
increasingly, it's false.

Ten months of Keats
fly out the window.

*

Bone in the throat: a hard wound to lick.

*

What's a year of silence
less, or more?

*

Regard it as a friend, i.e.,
an extension —
            what you'd do if
you had been there.

Lost Source,
   make the world your own.
Thirst the sky absorbs,
   clouds on deserts.

*

Song's metaphysic
may be breath:

one deep breath
and now another.

*

Wind alone on the hill
holds back.

Hoarding pain the planet's had enough of.

*

Walls don't separate people.
Neither do words.
Consciousness does that.

*

On lawn chairs
in Papa's garden
I sit beside you
            racing.

Doreen Stock

JUST THIS DAY FROM THE BEAUTIFUL SUN

water　　sun　　air
our bodies inhabited by silver
our blood rolling
like marbles on a wooden floor

the sun sliding thru the window
your mouth is
now it is your tongue
under such morning air
such waves
that only seem to be water

crime falls apart in the streets
like a cask of jewels

children turn cartwheels in slow motion

the trees are burning from their
roots in rainbows　　I can taste them

the dead the living leap
from their shadows
gray stones soft
and easily laughing

ISLAND

your old man, my old woman
they meet over our heads
they kiss, rain down bread
to be our bodies

their old hands crumble something

it is the earth, whole and stained
and spins under us

far off, a voice singing
a passionate voice
too beautiful to hear

it gives itself land and water

it tears the seagull's wing
out of the stormraw air

THE UNICORN

We're driving up highway 5 from LA
and her brother and sister have finally
fallen asleep. It's hot in the back seat
and it's a long ride.

Her mother and father are not speaking.
The road is brown.

The last unicorn is turning its white
shoulder with delicate sadness in someone's
dream.

Her eyes are filled with light.
She raises them from this book
and laughs.

"They say this is just fantasy!" she says

In June she will be ten years old.

WHO BY FIRE, WHO BY WATER

its in the corner we turn
your story rising in palms
like a sacred ditty

oh I've heard it so many times
before: the bones, the blood, the fire
but this so pale and gently smells
of smoke

that the beautiful charred feathers
do cling to your arms like shadows
that your father's voice does stretch
its backstreet down to the waters
its oilblack lines do float out
from the shore

singing that islands ring
of impossible voices
that books fall open
that long transparent fingers
stain themselves into knots

shatter themselves in glass rooms

that there be weeping like the wrong Madonna
laughter like love   silence
like prayers opening their own white walls
until gold splashes them down

and I taste the ancient breastbone
cracked apart   in harps and marrows
of light

that I must leave you
sundown in your arms
the sidewalk to put your foot to
the evening sky
glowing   vacant   shells of endless
aching hands

and that we hear the last sounds
silver bells
in tails of the oldest fishes

they swirl behind your throat
and give you
what you have needed to begin

MORE

I am the unseen
the grey mist where your heart
knows itself anywhere

I am the time that draws
its own circles in your flesh
the thread that will not rip
the beast that always turns
in the sun
the low fireyellow moon
rocking the night in its belly

I am the hill with your arms
floating on its back
where your root spreads itself
thick with a silver you've been keeping

I am land and water
I am your only words
I am the darkness holding your breath
as you give it

VOICE 2

you come to me in others now
your mouth has grown its white leaves

someone
a cough catch at the back of my throat
silence of the dead who will not die you slip
thru my night like colored water

white mountains, the still small sound
echoing among their shoulders

you

you ugliness you terror you despair
you lips pulled back grim

you tear
you hollow bell

even that i put my hand to
"here" I say and put my teeth
to your jaw

years later we speak
we're always speaking

William Pitt Root

DREAMING THE SHARK, WAKING THE DREAM

That grim hoop,
   hinged and toothed and terrible
jawbone of the great white shark who passes
like a shock
   along the deepest current in our dream,
how harmless waking renders it,
this mobile hung by wires in the air.
No danger in it,
none.

     Except
that as we wake the dream wake, too,
the spirit wake. Except
that then as the head grows back and body back
   to propel it, a sea
just warm enough to sustain that cold
   blood suddenly surrounds and buoys it
again and that a vessel passes
   over on currents led to it and
then that we, dazed
   by the sun and spectral moon
the ship sails through, slide
from the bow, slowly
   as in a dream, given
into waves where we must float half in
   the world of air, half in the water,
with no wish for the ship to turn,
no wish to drown.

Blinking in the blur of the light
   our lashes drip, we must desire
our lives and live embracing
   and embraced by water
as we breathe, swimming, waiting,
saving one coherent cry
   against the first sign of the fin
that slits, foaming, from trough to wavetip,
trough to wavetip toward us, circling,
   never losing the scent. And if
     on the first pass
it misses

   it must come back, it must
remember to come back, must
   not fear us for our kicking
nor for thrashing half up out of water,
   nor, drug under,
for seeking with blind hands across
the monumental face for the flat
   eyes incapable of closure.

Must take us,
must not let go although we wake
   from our dream, it from its,
and all that we have become dissolves
   into that single resolution
a wakeful sea shall render gaunt, blind, dead,
reduce to one grim smile of bone
   drifting the lightless
sea-miles down in an abyss too cold,
   too far and dark, for even
the most relentless light's formal reflection.

LEARNING PRAYER AMONG STONES

To speak to rock
is to become rock,
whose mouth
is the gradual utterance
of sand
upon tongues of water
and the wind.
Is to be blind
to the nightvoid
and dayvoid
of the moon and sun.
Reflections, origin:
Eyes of the owl
deep in saguaro
in the ghost of a sea,
eyes of the iguana
set in the sparkle
of a living surf.
Deaf. Numb to the cleavages
and crumbling of self.
To not speak.
To remain
among stones
a stone.

SONG OF SALT AND THE GALE

Arched waves hit the rocks
and arc up cliffs
like flame, and flecks
of spume blown inland
on the pale level wind
speckle the wild carrots
and the grass.
                          Here
slow cloudlike sheep and mares
with colts on stilts
and does attending
sky-eyed fawns
gather along the sea
at dawn, licking and grazing
where odors of spindrift
rise like sunlight from a living dew.

Sandra Kovacs

AFTER SEPARATION AND RETURN

After this short time apart
the slight touching of lips you insist upon as you leave
betrays the beast that
sits rocklike
at the very edge of your canyon.

How relieved I am
to know that my dirty burden disappears
with the dirty hope that led you to believe
in my passion;
that has tainted my skin
clogged my pores.

Each day you are gone I remove layers of hope in me
Layers of knowing that I couldn't
The groans that wouldn't come
The shuck of beauty that captured its own beast
The wolf that ran behind each night as I walked
reminding
silently
to go to bed to fail.

PING PONG

As if all learning has deceived us,
left us naked as kings before babes,
we meet on this dark green field,
animals to wrestle with the white foe
in some ancient anger.

If the mind could blink it would lose all thinking
as the eyes do.
White stain fixes to the eye, obscuring all
but its own weightless danger
and even as it is yanked cleverly behind
eye sees
flicks the tongue quick beyond the field
whips it back
unmistakeably out of reach of that vicious mouth.
No, it spits back.

I am one long willowed snake body striking
whose tongue knows only white click, white click
and when I miss or hit wild into the bush
I wonder at this tongue, why it has shamed me.

HARVEST

Always it is the promise
of plump yellow corn shucked, steaming
pressing sweetly in my teeth
that draws me here.
Of green tomatoes becoming palpable and red
and long beans hanging.
Of the magic glints of sun that whip me from your eyes
of onions torn hot from their beds
of fingers touching, letting go
waiting
waiting sweetly for the harvest.

ON THE DEATH OF MY GRANDMOTHER

Blessed is the meek
who sent a dollar in a card on my birthdays.

Grandma, I never saw you cry
but your lip trembled that way.
The girl inside my muscles still wants your soft, quick hug
to tighten
to show me how old women feel.
Grandma, winter couldn't wait for you.
Now you lie scattered in a small shiny box
for the rest of our seasons
hoping we will think you out
share some dreams with you.

We are the sturdy ones, the end of summer ones.
Stiff, tall cornstalks in the field to feed the hungry and the weak.
Spring ones admire us.
Old ones lean against us.
We shade the young and tender.

You were tired, I know you were tired.

As each season goes leaving no space
but a new wind, a new sun
even as water flows and never broken
passes strange holes and rocks more deep, or wide, or thin,
we let you go, knowing how soon we follow.

Diane Fabric

BATH, 7 A.M.

This was not my intention
  but intent has little to do
    with what goes on.

Poppies were still asleep
  when I caught my runaway horse
  in the silent, songless fog
    just after dawn.

This blurry morning —
  crawling back out of the night,
  lugging a wounded mountain along . . .

I'm unready for this sun.
I'll leave the curtain closed
  for now
and bathe awhile
  before the mist is gone.

SUNDAY, BEAR VALLEY

We hiked along the fault line —
  you, I, and the child —
touched moss,
  smelled the earth,
    watched insects in the sun.
I denied the tremors
  that have stopped me in the night
  to listen to the pounding of my heart.
Finishing our kiss,
  I laughed and stomped upon the ground
and dared the earth to move
  another sixteen feet.

MORNING DRIVE EAST

Nets of dew
  on raspberry branches
capture the sun
  for awhile
until the prey
  dissolves the glimmers
that grace its bonds.

I fly in and out of light,
  between the trees,
  beneath the fog.

Swinging around the curves,
  dodging quail on the valley road,
I realize
  there are no decisions to make.
The water flows,
  the mountain erodes.

Single heron,
  gracing the reservoir;
black and white cows
  on the hills:
these are my gifts from the morning
to carry me through the day.

DEFYING THE FOG

I don't need to be shown the signs.
I know the way down
    by heart.

Shaking this gloom of moons,
    I rise to fill my lungs
and meet your eyes.
October sun so sweet I ache
    (how I've come to hate the cold) —
orange gently torn and shared at noon:
    unexpected freshness
    to my thirst.

I send you flower-thoughts
    through morning mist
and thanks.

POINT REYES

My place is in these low and loping hills,
    with sweet dry earth
        and spicy chaparral,
    long-leaved, crying trees
        and lines of cypress.

Majestic ridge,
    holding back the fog;
long, silent valley,
    bearing an awesome power . . .

This place evokes a hush,
    a letting go
        of insignificance.

Your eyes probe the deepest corners
        of this night —
are there dreams you won't abandon
        in the darkened, distant faces
                blurred with pain?

Tender touch,
        solid need —
your strength explodes:
        falling midnight star,
poet,
        restless streak of beauty
                in the night,
        singer
                of lost
                and silent dreams.

The intensity
        of talks past midnight:
some desparate hope
        for a prevention of pain,
a recognition
        of ice
                on the curve . . .

The water:
I can see movement,
but not knowing if it is the wind
        or the tide,
I cannot tell the danger
        or the depth.

I awaken early:
        poised suspension
                between the flight
        and the fall.

HAIKU

These are my days without you —
        memory
                like saltwater
        to my thirst.

The wide,
        expectant void —

like an afternoon canyon
        without a hawk

Winding down the mountain into fog:
    the highway home.
Grass and horse tails
    blowing in the wind
and wildflowers,
    blooming brilliant by the road,
seduce my eyes.
I long to see you.
Stars warn us of the danger of these days.
Tenacity
    is our task:
        managing to breathe
            while clinging to the ledge —
mastering
    the curves
        of the descent.

GOING HOME

Though a year's made little change,
    I feel a toll.
We know the ritual well —
    no stumbling here,
        merely occasional pauses of the heart —
shocked suspensions in silence —
    disbelief.

I know the time to forget.
I feel it acutely
    at dawn.
Clarity takes time.
Such things seem incidental,
    hurtling through fog.

Poppies
    are all asleep
except for one
    bright
        insomniac
eyeing the dusk . . .

JANUARY NIGHT, ROUTE 1

Fog enfolds us now
and orange highway markers
    are all we have to guide us
    around the cliff-top curves
      above the sea.

Houselights
    like tiny stars
twinkle through the night,
assuring me that warmth
    can come again.

John Francis

I left that morning
amid handshakes and tears;
hastily spoken words,
hesitating only to shift the load.

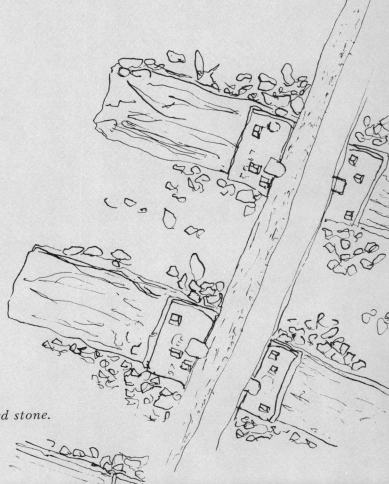

And while the grey fog lay thick
behind brown hills,
I walked along the tracks
stepping from tie to tie
not counting
heels crunching on grey oil splotched stone.

The whistle wailed
the locomotive passed
with clacking wheels and rattling boxcars,
the engineer smiling
waved as I sat in the grass
by the drawbridge
lost in some old banjo riff
waiting to cross the river.

Gleaming rails fading into a roadside dream
morning comes with the dripping of fog from green slick needles
and the dull crash of the surf
against a white splattered rock
the seagull with one maimed leg
limps across a picnic table
and flies off.

At the old fort
archeologists dig and measure
in hopes of uncovering;
rediscovering the present.
The sound of automobiles passing
mingled with that of the sea.
Crys of a hunting osprey
and our own breath making ghostly vapors in cool morning air.

It was a wedding
and I played all day reflecting in new faces
as we walked through redwoods to the meadow for the ceremony.
We all witnessed:
   "If I have all these things but have not loved. . ."
There was dancing through the trees,
bride and groom running hand and hand
all growing closer as the day grew older,
the moon, still growing had risen,
the tree swayed and the sea splashed
silver on a rocky shore.

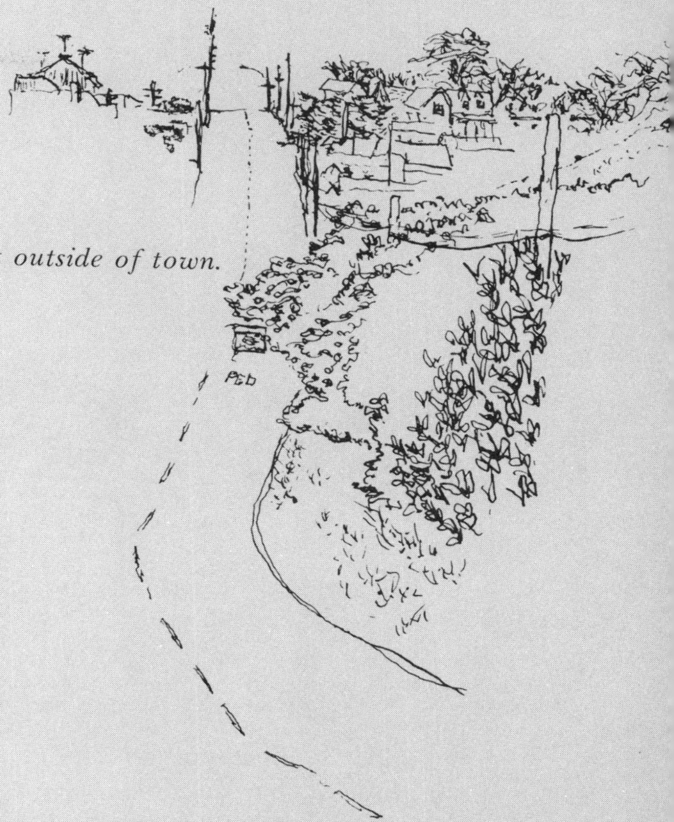

The rain was falling as I walked down
the main street,
just enough to make the windshield wipers
work on all the cars that went by
and enough to make me stop under some cypress trees just outside of town.
By the river I gratefully accepted
the shelter of a bridge for the night,
prepared my meal while the rain
made circles in the flowing water,
a foghorn bellowed in the distance
sadly.

Morning was filled
with all new smells,
wet and heavy
hanging in the air.
The cows passed along the swollen river,
trees appeared out of silvery grey mist
and then were gone.

I stopped again to visit friends
and fill a little round house with silent song and sleep,
letting some tired miles finally slip
away,
listening to the ocean roar below.

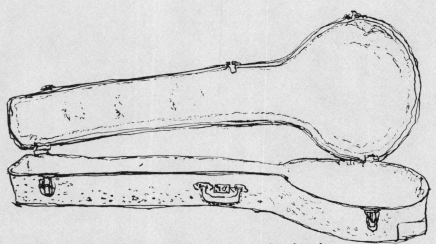

Then there was another crowd of clapping hands,
bright lights and a stage,
so I played awhile my favorite banjo tunes
and after I had shared all of my dreams,
stepped out into the night to find some more.

Through another door as if it were not there
to walk along the beach collecting wood
watching a lone sea lion playing in the surf
remembering their barking along the way
and brown furry bodies dotting sun-drenched rocks.
The moon rose full.

I climbed with the highway the very next day,
leaving a cool ocean dream behind.
Ridges stretched out beyond one another
while air conditioned motor homes passed
with the rest of sunday's traffic.

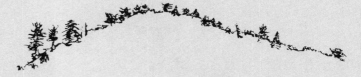

The moon getting smaller now
each day sinking behind the trees
before the sun rises above the mountains.

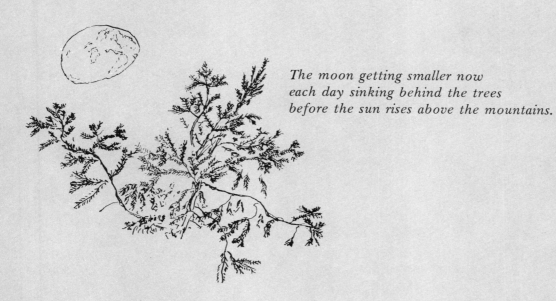

And the road flows beside the river
and quietly through the redwood groves
where I am obliged to pause and be;
walk among the trees;
quiet giants;
spirits of my dream.

Among the trees rain comes again
and shelter is offered inside the
heart of an old friend
shared with the owls and the squirrels
scratching circles in the river.

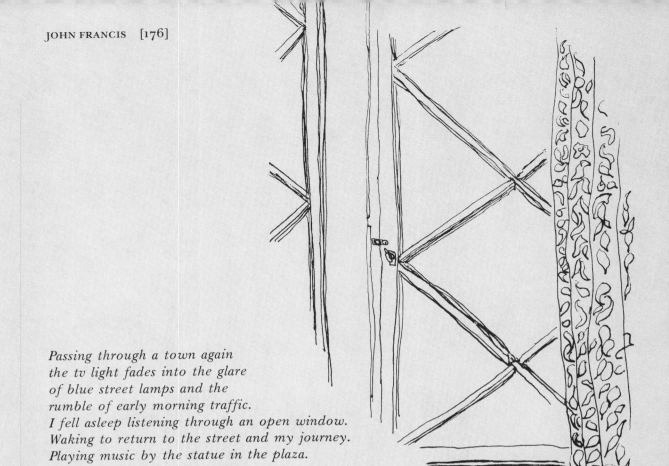

Passing through a town again
the tv light fades into the glare
of blue street lamps and the
rumble of early morning traffic.
I fell asleep listening through an open window.
Waking to return to the street and my journey.
Playing music by the statue in the plaza.

Another night of searching in the dark,
stumbling through the woods,
sliding down banks, barking dogs,
an invitation, the door open, the light on,
but I slept across the road where the
old trees had fallen and the new
ones had sprung forth all around.
A million stars blazing coldness in
a black night.

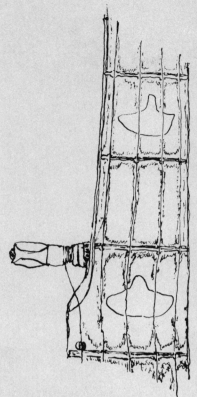

Still lightly touching steel strings
following the music and laughing silently
dissolving into the movement of tone
time and the road.

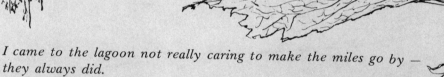

I came to the lagoon not really caring to make the miles go by —
they always did.
Laying beneath the leaves of the trees
watching the fog arrive in great white patches,
playing the banjo quietly as sparrows sat
singing near by with a stubby little owl
letting the smoke from the fire drift lazily
into the air.

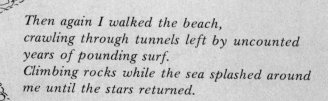

Then again I walked the beach,
crawling through tunnels left by uncounted
years of pounding surf.
Climbing rocks while the sea splashed around
me until the stars returned.

Passing along the coast

through the last few crowded towns until

the road becomes

the path.

NOTES ON CONTRIBUTORS

MORGAN ALEXANDER   left Woodstock for the West Coast where she is presently engaged in stimulating research somewhere in the mountains north of Los Angeles.

DOUGLAS BLAZEK   "I have come to write out of my life, its peculiar characteristics that energy manifests as it forms into a human seed. I write toward my elucidation, toward that which has not yet solidified in me to my agreement. My flaws. That strata of rock rumbling and slipping under pressure."

ROBERT BLY   These versions of poems by Kabir, a fifteenth-century Indian, are rendered from previous translations by Rabindranath Tagore, assisted by Evelyn Underhill, and published by Macmillan. Bly: "I simply put a few of them, whose interiors I had become especially fond of, into more contemporary language, to see what they might look like."

ADRIAN BROOKS   lives in San Francisco where he plays in the fields of the Lord with the Angels of Light.

ED BURYN   describes himself as "a writer, photographer, publisher, landlord, half-time parent, and vagabond eccentric." A San Franciscan for the past sixteen years, he has written three books: *Hitchhiking in Europe, Vagabonding in Europe and North Africa,* and *Vagabonding in America.* He is also the photographer for the book *Two Births* which documents the birth of his daughter, Sierra.

RAY COSSEBOOM   lives in Boston. Writes: "Michael, you know where we are heading: black holes, nebulas, a 90,000 mile tower beyond our solar system. Before long: communication with extraterrestrial intelligence. Before long: it will be realized we are all weightless. Knock, knock."

LAWRENCE FERLINGHETTI   Ferlinghetti's most recent book is *Who Are We Now?* published by New Directions, which includes the two poems in this edition of *Floating Island.*

MIKE FINLEY   The Minnesota Writer's Publishing House will publish Finley's new book, tentatively titled *Anton's Syndrome. Lucky You,* a book of poems, has been published by Litmus Inc of Salt Lake City.

JOHN FRANCIS   walks everywhere he goes with backpack and banjo, has maintained a vow of silence for years now, but will sometimes whistle, laugh, sing in the voice of birds. Recent postcard from Shakespeare Festival in Ashland, Oregon: "Shakespeare. Just great. Laughing and crying, getting lost in another period that somehow connects with the present. After a long hot walk up the Sacramento Valley (a new way for me) meeting a million people, spirits, climbed Mt. Shasta (took away all my breath). Now on my way to the wilderness."

FRANK GRAZIANO   Born in Oceanside, New York, in 1955, he is presently an undergraduate at the University of Arizona and employed by the Arizona Poets-in-the-Schools Program. In 1975 he founded, and at present continues to edit, the literary journal *Grilled Flowers.*

JUDITH ANNE GREENBERG   lives in Mendocino, California. Her work has appeared in numerous magazines, including *The Nation, Works, Western Humanities Review,* and *Southern Poetry Review.* She has also had two chapbooks published: *Fire in August* from Zeitgeist Press and *Fields of Light* from Casseopeia Press.

BOBBIE LOUISE HAWKINS   will have a new book of stories, *Frenchie and Cuban Pete and Other Stories,* published by Tombouctou Books of Bolinas in 1977.

DANA CHRISTIAN JENSEN   is presently teaching creative writing and tribal folk theater at Intermountain Intertribal School in Brigham City, Utah. After his work there he will return to the snowiest parts of Minnesota.

SANDRA KOVACS   lives in Mill Valley, California, makes and sells batik clothing and paintings, raises chickens, works in her garden to grow with her two children, even at times putting everything aside for a few days to write.

JOANNE KYGER   reads the legends of the Hookooeko aloud, her hands fluttering like birds in the lamplit, fog-drifted downtown evening of Bolinas, California.

EUGENE LESSER lives in the fashionable resort of his own back yard, just down the road from Woodacre, California. The poems in this edition of *Floating Island* are taken from the infamous and as yet unpublished manuscript *Drug Abuse in Marin County*, originally entitled *Mondo Woodacre*.

JONATHAN LONDON lives in San Francisco where he works in a bookstore in Noe Valley. His poems have appeared in *Quasar, Isthmus, Invisible City, Lamp in the Spine,* and *Kyoi/Kuksu*. He "was once a dancer, am a dancer, will always be a traveler (going to Greece next Spring, went to South America last Spring)."

HELEN NESTOR lives and works in Berkeley and Inverness. The photographs in this edition of *Floating Island* are from her journals.

JOHN READ is the author of a house and the father of a school which appeared suddenly in Point Reyes Station.

WILLIAM PITT ROOT writes from Brer Truck enroute from Portland, Oregon, through Mendocino and Yuma to Lafayette, Louisiana: "These are poems from *Faultdancing*, which will be my fourth book if ever it becomes a printed book at all. *Coot & Others: A Book of Characters* will come out of Confluence Press next summer; *The Storm* and *Striking the Dark Air for Music* came from Antheneum."

DALE SAMOKER was born 2/25/50 in Minneapolis, emigrated to Inverness three years ago, recently returned from a journey to Bolivia.

ARAM SAROYAN recently published a book of his poems, *O My Generation and Other Poems*, under his own imprint of Blackberry Books. He lives with his wife Gailyn and their three children in northern California.

GINO CLAYS SKY flies down from the north country where he edited *Wild Dog* with Ed Dorn in Pocatello, Idaho, in the early sixties. Books published include *Sweet Ass'd Angels, Pilgrims, and Boogie Woogies* from Cranium Press and *Jonquil Rose* from Five Trees Press.

DOREEN STOCK lives in Mill Valley, California, where she coordinates the poetry readings at the Mill Valley Book Depot. She has published translations from the Russian.

MICHAEL SYKES found an extraordinary symbol on the slopes of Mount Shasta in September, 1969, during the main course of a three-day fast.

PAT URIOSTE lives in northern Virginia and edits the Feedback Column for Len Fulton's *Small Press Review*. Her work has been published in *Shameless Hussy Review, Illuminations, Puddingstone,* and *River Bottom,* among others.

PAUL WEAR lives in San Francisco and was co-editor (with Luke Breit) of *Beatitude 24*.

JAMES L. WHITE is published widely in little magazines, and has three books of poetry: *Divorce Proceedings* from University of South Dakota Press, *A Crow's Story of Deer* from Capra Press, and *The Del Rio Hotel* from Dacotah Territory Press. He is presently teaching at an Indian school in Utah, on a grant provided by the Utah State Division of Fine Arts.

A.D. WINANS is the editor of *Second Coming* and of Second Coming Press, which recently published *California Bicentennial Poets Anthology*.

MICHAEL WOLFE lives in Bolinas and is the editor and publisher of Tombouctou Books. A book of his poems, *World Your Own,* will be published soon by Calliope Press of Walpole, New Hampshire.

CHRISTINE ZAWADIWSKY is Ukranian, born New York City, now living in Milwaukee "with my parrot, Rico, and I've kept wild animals in the past—a raccoon, a meadowlark, a sparrow, others. Birds and wild animals fascinate me." She is doing translations from the Ukranian and was a National Endowment recipient in poetry last summer.

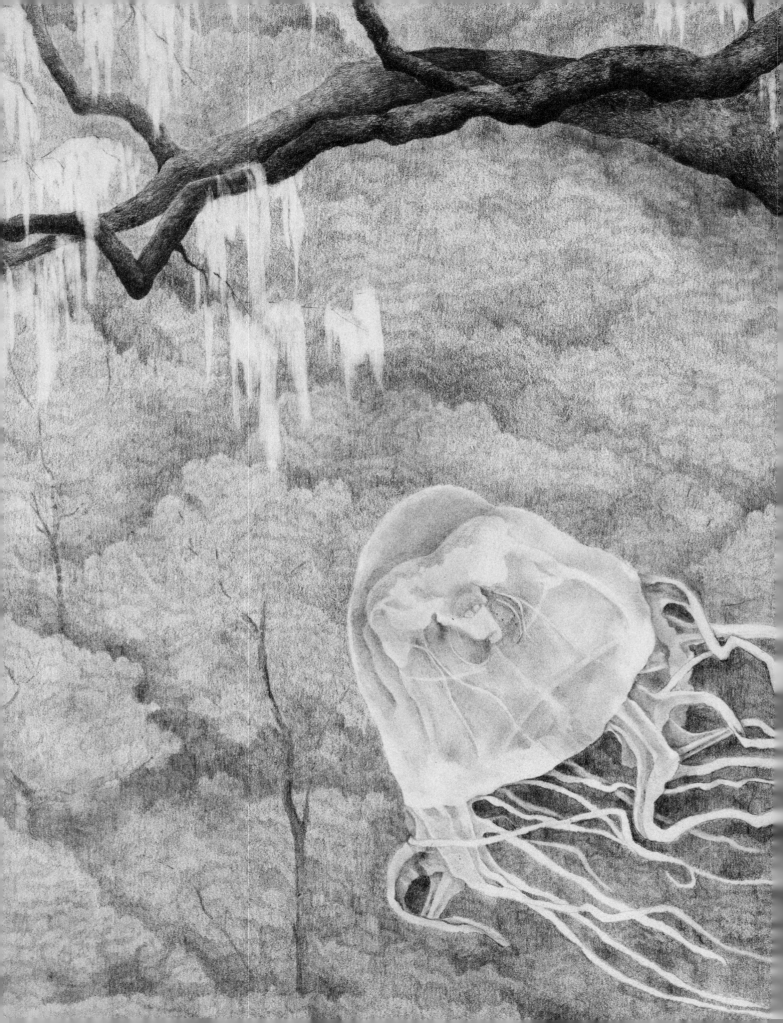

Each wave
driven cliffward
blasts to foam
against the rocks,
consumes the gnarling
roots of trees
whose upper branches
vanish into mist.

Below the waves
glide creatures
feeding and serene.

Above mist
shines the daystar,
constant in oceanic air.

—William Pitt Root
Song of the Levels

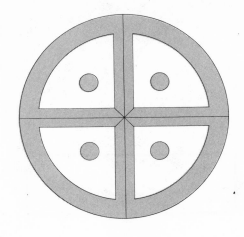

Floating Island

**The following recipe was handed to me on the run by Drew Allen as we passed on the
bridge over Papermill Creek in Point Reyes Station.** —*MS*

The custard:
1 quart milk
1 cup sugar
1 vanilla bean
10 egg yolks
grated rind of ½ lemon

The islands:
4 egg whites
1 small pinch salt
1 small pinch cream of tartar
1 ½ cups sifted powdered sugar

Bring the milk, sugar, and vanilla to a boil in a low, wide pan. Remove from the flame and leave
the vanilla bean to steep while preparing the meringue islands. Add the salt and cream of tartar to
the egg whites and beat them until they form stiff peaks; then sift over the powdered sugar,
folding it in easily but thoroughly. Take the vanilla bean from the milk, bring milk to a second
boil, and maintain it at a bare simmer.

Gently place a heaping teaspoon of the uncooked islands into the milk, being careful not to
crowd. (The islands swell as they cook.) After a few minutes, turn them over and leave them to
poach a few minutes more. When done, remove them with a slotted spoon and allow to drain on a
nylon sieve over a mixing bowl. When drained, put them into a large and deep serving platter to
make room for the rest. When all the islands have been poached and drained, pour the poaching
milk through the sieve to join what is already there. Beat the egg yolks, add the lemon rind, and
slowly pour in the milk, continuing to whisk. Pour the mixture into a heavy saucepan over a low
flame, stirring and scraping the sides constantly with a wooden spoon until the mixture coats the
spoon. Do not allow to boil.

When the custard is done, remove it from the heat immediately, pour it through the sieve into
another bowl and then pour it carefully into the serving platter, around but not over the islands.
Chill, and garnish with berries.